MASTER OF DECEPTION

A SON SEARCHES FOR HIS FATHER IN THE HOUSE OF ILLUSION

MASTER OF DECEPTION

John-Ivan Palmer

RARE BIRD
LOS ANGLES. CALIF.

THIS IS A GENUINE RARE BIRD BOOK

Rare Bird Books
453 South Spring Street, Suite 302
Los Angeles, CA 90013
rarebirdbooks.com

FIRST HARDCOVER EDITION

Set in Dante
Printed in the United States

10 9 8 7 6 5 4 3 2 1

Library of Congress Cataloging-in-Publication Data

Names: Palmer, John-Ivan, author.
Title: The master of deception : a son searches for his father in the house
of illusion / John-Ivan Palmer.
Description: First hardcover edition. | Los Angeles : Rare Bird Books, 2020.
Identifiers: LCCN 2020019626 (print) | LCCN 2020019627 (ebook) | ISBN
9781644281437 (hardback) | ISBN 9781644281499 (epub)
Subjects: LCSH: Palmer, John-Ivan—Family. | Hypnotists—United
States--Biography.
Classification: LCC BF1127.P35 A3 2020 (print) | LCC BF1127.P35 (ebook) |
DDC 793.8/092 [B]—dc23
LC record available at https://lccn.loc.gov/2020019626
LC ebook record available at https://lccn.loc.gov/2020019627

For my mother and father and Harue

History has many cunning passages, contrived corridors
with whispering ambitions.

—T. S. Eliot, *Gerontion*

THE INTRO

MY FATHER ALWAYS STOOD out as someone "not from around here." He walked the streets of small-town America in stage makeup, clear nail polish, and a pencil-thin mustache framing a crocodilian smile that made him look, it was said, like "he had a million teeth." His legs were not like other legs. They were so bowed he had to wear specially tailored pants with cuffs that broke neatly over shoes polished to draw attention from a distance, the way he was usually seen, even up close. He made a strong first impression, but as a second impression he didn't seem to be there at all. Left-handed, he trained himself to pull cards out of the air with his right. The cards came from somewhere on the far side of his hand, but, like him, they appeared to come from nowhere.

My father was a man of secrets, and his burden weighed just as heavily on me and my mother. The public got the smile, but in longer intervals between performances he sat in our trailer robotically practicing card tricks with a bug-eyed stare and let his whiskers grow out. I was always intensely curious about him but he was "not from around here" even when at home. So I studied what he kept in his pockets, glove compartment, shaving bag, suitcase. But those objects revealed little more than a man who traveled extremely light. He was the trick I would have to figure out.

OPENING ACT

STRANGER IN THE HOUSE

THOSE OF US WHO live outside of arbitrary norms are easily subject to caricature—sombrero, watermelon, flied lice, lederhosen, moneybags. They stick, and they are hard to unstick. Utter the word "magician" and it immediately falls into the grip of stereotype, with the top hat and cape (which he never wore) and the wand (which he never used). My father didn't float my mother or saw her in half, although he did occasionally lock her in a box and instantly switch places with her. He picked pockets, did a memory stunt, produced a few birds, made jokes, and shook a giant New Zealand white rabbit in a woman's face to make her scream while he grinned with all of those teeth. On the practical side, to commodify and sell his brand of downscale variety, typecasting had to be used as a token of trade, like the "lovely assistant" (my mother) and "the rabbit big as a St. Bernard" (that never came from a hat). He was part of a Sargasso Sea of public unknowns who traveled the country like Paul Rosini, Tung Pin Soo (Al Wheatley), Russell Swann, Mardoni and Louise, Doc Irving and Princess Yvonne, George Marquis, Hathaway, Gloria Gerome, Jack Herbert, Bob Parker, Virgil the Magician, Plato and Jewell.

Ring any bells? Precisely.

Nabokov once wrote that he detested floor shows. They were beneath his refined sensibilities. Philip Carey, Maugham's alter ego in *Of Human Bondage*, looked down with "scornful eyes" on "conjurers and trick-cyclists." In "The Circus Animals' Desertion" Yeats called his inferior work a kind of act on a "painted stage" featuring the "stilted boys" and "the Lord knows what." They were not real people but "emblems" from his "rag-and-bone shop," with the implication that variety performers are something "mere," an adjective predictably paired with the word "entertainment."

As a mandatory member of the American Guild of Variety Artists (AGVA), my father was part of a vast post-War industry known as "variety entertainment." AGVA was a division of the American Federation of Labor and regulated the industry tightly. After World War II, people's attention was still uncaptured, and there was profit to be made from a culture starved for amusement in thousands of fraternal halls, nightclubs, hotels, and fairgrounds throughout the US and Canada. Fred Smith of the old Al Sheehan Agency in Minneapolis, one of my father's many bookers, told me, "Acts are canned goods. Here's your corn, here's your peas. I sell 'em, you buy 'em." Of course, no one buys that kind of stuff anymore. Times have changed and floor shows have gone the way of car fins and westerns. When the day came for Smith to close shop, he cleared out four file cabinets of eight-by-ten publicity photos from a time when stages were ubiquitous and there was a regulated industry to keep them lit. Assuming a hundred glossies per inch, the total storage capacity of his four file cabinets would be five hundred and sixty linear inches—which comes to about eight thousand photos. Sure, there were files with multiple photos—brochures, newspaper and magazine reviews—plus the thickness of the folders themselves, so even if ten percent of that number represented individual performers, that's a lot of dead souls traveling continuously day and night across North America.

The Sheehan Agency, like the others, followed strict AGVA union rules. Engagement contracts had to be in standard form, typed in quadruplicate with copies kept by the client, the act, the agent, and the union office. AGVA had big clout. Union spies went to hotels and clubs all over the country to make sure that every tap dancer, hand balancer, and cigarette swallower was a paid-up member. If not, the agent, the performer, and the venue would be blacklisted, and no other union members would be allowed to work with them for risk of being blacklisted themselves. Livelihoods were at stake. If one juggled apples while eating them, made a chimp ride a bicycle, hung by their teeth, tap danced with a peg leg, sang "Danny Boy," or pulled cards out of the air, they belonged to AGVA or they did not work. To be accepted as a member they had to be sponsored by two AGVA agents in good standing whose very existence depended on the ability of their performers to make a competent showing in places no one had ever heard of.

In the 1950s people physically interacted with each other a great deal more than they do today, possibly from the exhilaration of simply being alive after so many millions had died in the War. They belonged to organizations and clubs of all kinds. Banquets were frequent and floor shows were the custom. At theatrical agencies, phones rang constantly asking for performers. Someone from the Fraternal Order of Elks in Grand Forks might call the Shehan Agency in Minneapolis and say they had a $300 budget. Smith would say, "I can open the show for you with Tony Ragini, who does a nice juggling act; then Mirna Tell on accordion, followed by the Human Pretzel; then Professor Merrill, who does a funny bit with a trombone; and close with the Master of Deception, who pulls a gigantic rabbit out of thin air and shakes it in a woman's face until she screams and pees in her pants. Dynamite stuff. I can throw in a five-piece orchestra and you've got a helluva show within your budget. Where should I send the contract?" He'd write down the address, hand it to his secretary, then take the next call. Twenty to fifty dollars an engagement was considered good money, but it didn't go very far, so my father and those like him never turned down an offer, no matter how low the pay or how far the drive. That meant a life of constant travel.

I grew up in dressing rooms with the likes of Tom Gary ("Comedy a la Mode"), Billy Papon ("The Prince of Pantomime"), a talking dog, an alcoholic knife thrower, a risqué ventriloquist, and assorted burlesque dancers like the Daring Lovadis and the Human Heat Wave. I was trained to be invisible around them since no one wants a kid in a dressing room, but I saw and heard everything. Sometimes I spied on the famous like Sophie Tucker, Hopalong Cassidy, and Clarabell the Clown. I had my chores, like retrieving the doves that flew off the stage, shoveling mayflies away from the footlights, and repacking my father's props. Home was a trailer parked in towns I seldom knew the names of, and for education my father had me follow kids to school and simply walk in and take a seat.

The only home I knew was a three-thousand-pound Travelo pulled by a series of cars that were all worn out within a year. The props and my mother's possessions brought the weight up to at least a couple of tons. We pulled it in a slow and exhausting process from town to town and trailer park to trailer park. From the back seat I watched my father's growing exhaustion, as he stared at the road while day turned into night and then into day again, continually running his fingers through his magnificent wavy hair to stay awake. Every steering wheel on every car he owned was slick with hair oil. On roads glazed with ice or through rain, blizzards, or a windshield smeared with bugs, my mother and I relied on him to keep our moving estate from veering into the ditch.

•••

IF BRINGING KIDS ON family trips will test one's patience, try doing it as a way of life. Long periods of confinement are known to cause peculiar reactions in child, man, and beast. After a season or two of intense travel, my father's gigantic rabbit began biting out its own fur and eating it. Its working life would be around two years. The Java doves pecked each other's heads until they were bald. They didn't last much longer. As for myself, I formed a menagerie of private voices, male and female, that to this day still repeat the most absurd utterances to satisfy an inexplicable neural necessity. As the hours dragged on, the more intense my chanted repetitions became. Yet my father was surprisingly tolerant. He simply asked if I would not mind containing myself.

But I could not contain myself. I thought up ingenious ways to annoy my mother, already half-crazy from road fatigue, by tickling her ear with a dove feather or pushing up under her seat with my toes or tossing tiny bits of paper into her hair. The longer they remained in her hair without her noticing, the funnier it got. I'd hold back as long as I could, then burst out in laughter, which became as unstoppable as the private voices. Finally, my father would have no choice but to pull over at a playground to let me out.

"There's some kids! Hurry up and play!"

I always looked for children who were alone because I assumed they didn't have any friends either. At one such playground in some unknown town I approached a solitary boy who had merged two fantasies by wearing a pirate's hat and a toy six-gun. We hit it off immediately. He wanted to show me something, so I followed him down a ravine (what would kids have done without erosion?) and came upon a few boys gathered under a tangle of branches they'd made into a fort. Hanging from the branches were colorful bottles tied up with string, the rays of the setting sun filtering through them like stained glass in a church. Several kids were already there. One boy stood on an orange crate with his back to us, his pants down to his knees and his little white buttocks clenched as he thrust his hips forward. He tugged at something between his legs while a few of his friends watched. The pirate-cowboy ignored all that as he ran his hand through the bottles, jostling them together with a hollow sound like chimes. He said he put them up himself.

"Bigger boys come down here with baseball bats and smash the bottles, so watch out for glass on the ground."

Interrupted by our distraction, the boy on the crate brought his exhibition to a close, pulled up his pants, and said, "I can make it even bigger than that."

In the distance I heard my father's loud whistle. That was his signal for me to get back to the car. I scampered up the ravine and my friend followed. Our house on wheels rolled away before the pirate-cowboy could figure out who I was or where I'd come from or why I was there.

At least for the time being I remained quiet as we continued on the endless highway to my father's engagement, but inside my head the words kept repeating, *bigger than that...bigger than that...*

"Obsessive compulsive" might describe the condition, but it's a term, like "paranoid" and "schizo," that can apply to all sorts of behaviors on a spectrum within the normal range. Isolation may have nudged me a little further down the spectrum, but I never regarded it as anything to be concerned about, just something to live with. And I still do. It's only in idleness or boredom that the repetitions come out. I learned to control repeating thoughts by focusing my attention on memorizing whatever could be memorized: Burma Shave slogans, livestock breeds, entertainers' routines. Eventually I channeled this compulsion into books.

I have often thought that all it would take is a simple bump on the head to completely dislodge that loose screw and turn me into a muttering lunatic in want of forced confinement, which, ironically, is how it all started. The same obsessive state that originated in confinement in the back seat of a traveling magician's car would later motivate me to seek the answer to why he brought me and my mother into his hermetic world.

•••

THE FIRST THING MY father did after buying a new car was install a hitch. Then he took out the back seat and made a space for me on top of a folded blanket wedged between the bird and the rabbit cages. Thus, we were all caged together. After parking the trailer—often behind a gas station, as was common practice at the time—he set out for the local venue all smiles and charm in his darkened mustache and black fedora, cigarette hanging from his mouth, and accompanied by my mother in costume jewelry and redolent furs. He was big-time stuff in places like Newkirk, Huron, Milford, or Yates Center.

In the post-war boom, International Harvester Company, the farm implement dealer, promoted itself in small town America by advertising a "free family party" that promised "no sales talk, just entertainment." It was "the show you have been waiting for, your international hit parade, featuring stars of stage, radio, television," which were hundred-dollar-a-week commercial acts on highly organized tours called "units" set up by theatrical agents. There were seldom competing events, not even TV in many places, so attendance was guaranteed in the armory or high school auditorium to see the most eminent of the eminently unfamous, like Charlotte Allen ("Sweetheart of the West"), Billy Papon ("The Prince of Pantomime"), Jeane James ("Acrobatic Violinist"), Hal Plummer ("The Human Pretzel"), and Regini ("Europe's Greatest Juggler"), emceed by the "Master of Deception." First there was a promotional movie (in color!) of International Harvester tractors and harrows, hay balers, hoppers, and spreaders. Then there was the sixty-minute variety show. It was a folk event as deeply ingrained as the county fair. There were no two-story amplifiers and semi-trucks loaded with scaffolding. No fireworks, no multimedia razzle-dazzle. Just wardrobed human bodies with an uncommon skill placed in opposition to a crowd of viewers with nothing better to do. This was not fine art. An attractive woman in a sequined tutu balancing on a large glittery ball rolled up an incline was enough to make people glad they'd left the house. The simplest form of juggling was miraculous. Snapping a cigarette out of a female assistant's mouth with a bullwhip—astonishing. Pulling cards out of the air—unbelievable. Where else could you see such a thing but on that local stage on that wintry night?

•••

HE CREATED ENCHANTMENT IN places where enchantment was hard to come by, but he was incapable of experiencing it himself. If there was an interval when he was not providing amusement for others, he went into seclusion inside the trailer and bided his time practicing card manipulations at the drop-leaf table. His soul was in his fingers, struggling against their shortness. Like a concert pianist, he had to practice constantly to keep them limber for producing cards. This was especially important because his fingers were short and stubby, and although he was left-handed, he had to learn the difficult maneuvers from directions written for the right hand, as in this example from Annemann's *202 Methods of Forcing* (1933):

> When right hand with deck pulled up left sleeve, the bottom card of deck was easily spotted. Asking the party if they are satisfied, a pass is made and card brought to about two-thirds down in pack. A slight break is held at this point. The thumb of left hand now runs the cards of the upper portion, fanwise, over into the right hand, the person being, at the same time, invited to take one. When about half of the upper portion has been passed, a card, not the one to be forced, is pushed temptingly forward...

When he was a child in Rockport, Indiana, it was believed that left-handedness was a degenerate aberration, possibly Satanic, and so when he began school, his teacher tied his left hand down and forced him to use only his right. This resulted in a maladroit ambidexterity where he ate with his left hand but wrote with his right, and neither very well. His handwriting was a hybrid of print and cursive. Every time he applied himself to something manual, he had to fumble for whichever hand seemed appropriate for the task. Rather than translate sleight of hand directions to the left hand, it was easier to learn the means of enchanting others with his right and inure himself to constant practice.

For my mother, enchantment was another matter entirely. To her, anything could take on magical qualities. Her sense of wonder could be set off by a barbed-wire fence coated with ice. But when my father tapped his watch to indicate time was ticking, her enchantment disappeared and he went on her list of things that were not enchanting, like bugs, slovenly dress, psychiatrists, contortionists, drunkards, and any sexually suggestive female. And secrets. She hated secrets most of all. And that was what my father was. A walking secret. A card behind the hand. A sealed envelope.

"What is this and why is it here?" he often asked, referring to her many stray something-or-others. He could just as well have asked the same of himself, or me, or all three of us together. Or life in general.

Her reply was always, "You sound like a broken record." And if there actually were a broken record, she would have saved it along with everything else, like his route sheets with long lists of dates and towns. Those fourth and fifth carbon copies typed on onionskin by a theatrical agent are the only evidence I have that I grew up in Fowler, Ashland, Hugoton, Medicine Lodge, and Kiowa one week, and Turpin, Dodge City, Stafford, Pond Creek, Wellington, and Helena the next. Then off to Anthony, Cheney, Augusta, Moline, Newton, and Pratt, then on to Pretty Prairie, Sedan, Independence, Eureka, Cedarvale, and Neodesha, where we might layover in a trailer park, and I might even find a school to attend for a few days.

•••

IN MY FATHER'S WORLD, and therefore mine, there was no hometown, no neighborhood. We lived in no place and every place. In these far-flung towns, we weren't the only "Lord knows whats." Sometimes we'd end up for a few days in the same place as Billy Papon, "the Prince of Pantomime," or Tom Gary, who could bullwhip a dime off a bald man's head. We might be temporary neighbors with the Darryl Sisters, advertised as "real femininity dancing," or Hal Plummer, whose so-called human pretzel act came from his ability to pull his entire body through a tennis racket, or Frank Rains, the "Simul-talker," who could say anything you said at exactly the same time no matter how fast you spoke or tried to trip him up. We'd see them and they'd be gone, and maybe someday, some place, we'd see them again.

While my father was in the dressing room with the other performers, putting on his frock coat with studded cardboard front, I roamed like an Alice in a wide-ranging wonderland, exploring service elevators and stairways, loading docks and storage rooms. I had the run of America's banquet rooms, often themed as Italian villas or Tyrolean villages with ersatz alcoves and balconies forming imaginary worlds that were mine alone. There were Barcelona Suites, Palomino Halls, Port Royales, Savoys, Zanzibar Rooms, Moroccos, Auroras, Tivoli Gardens, Babalons. If anyone said anything to me, the magic words were *I'm with the show*. Then they'd leave me alone to explore other places I didn't belong. My friends were janitors, night watchmen, elevator operators, and cooks who gave me leftover tortes and parfaits.

They were as exotic to me as the Master of Deception was to them.

THEIR OWN PRIVATE STAGE

I HAVE SEEN MANY blizzards in the Midwest, mostly while traveling. To me they are not especially daunting. In fact, I'm rather comfortable being the only car on the road while everyone else is snowed in. In the hundred-below windchill and twenty-foot visibility I watch my old friends, the crows, on the roadside, going about their business, no more put off by the situation than I am.

One of my earliest memories of my father is seeing him digging our Hudson Hornet out of the snow in South Dakota. He was trying to pull our trailer through a blizzard to Ft. Pierre. It was an unspoken rule that canceling a show for any reason was unthinkable, so his efforts were especially desperate. As he worked metal treads under chained tires, the snow drifted up ever higher. The doves in the back seat next to me cawed away happily, as if they were still in the tropics of their native Java, and the rabbit could not have cared less. But my mother, who was supposed to pull the car forward without spinning the wheels, had her own way of seeing the situation. She was filming it with her eight-millimeter camera.

As a last resort he decided to unhitch the trailer and leave it in the grip of a giant snowdrift. That wasn't the only problem. There was me, the perfect reason why performer's kids (the nonperforming ones) either did not exist or were left safely elsewhere. To further complicate a complicated situation, I had a fever. At least that's the way my mother always told it. The choice was either all three of us continue to Ft. Pierre and risk getting stuck again and be at the mercy of how much gas remained in the tank, or leave me and my mother sheltered in the trailer while he went ahead and took the risk himself.

"I'll go ahead and come back for you," he said. "There's plenty of matches. Just light the stove. Pretty soon you'll be *too* warm." He got into the car, and with the birds crowing and the tire chains clacking, disappeared into the whiteout as if into a fading dream.

Inside the trailer, steam blew out my mother's mouth like clouds of dragon smoke as she prepared to light the stove where its flame would appear in the small Eisenglass window. There were indeed plenty of kitchen matches in the dispenser on the wall next to the stovepipe, but she made a horrifying discovery. In his rush to leave Prairie City, my father neglected to check the kerosene can, which was empty. That meant no heat.

Never leave your shelter is the age-old advice to survive a blizzard. We heard stories of people getting lost and freezing to death between a house and a barn, but my mother never paid attention to practical wisdom, preferring riskier tactics of her own. She tried to follow what she thought was the road back to the last town, carrying me as I hugged my stuffed Scottie, Sox. There was nothing to see because nothing was visible. All I remember is the smell of perfume on her fur coat as the violent winds swirled around us.

We could very well have ended up frozen solid until spring, but through a momentary breach in the swirling snow there appeared what looked like a shack. My mother banged on the door and a Native American woman answered. A couple of other women looked on as well as several children standing behind them. They recognized my mother as the magician's assistant from the night before at the Cavalcade of Stars show in the school gym. Before modernity overexposed and killed the mystery of novelty, any entertainer, no matter how lowly, carried a certain amount of prestige. Her showing up at their door in the middle of a blizzard was more miraculous than the stage show they saw the previous night. Maybe more so.

"Where's the magician?" one of the women asked.

"Who knows. He drove off to Ft. Pierre and left us in a trailer with no heat."

If such a situation reminded them of their dire historical past, they didn't show it as my mother entered their home with irrepressible screwball charm. I recall the house as a shack, but even a small shack would have seemed roomy compared to the living space we pulled behind us from town to town. Wind whistled in from all around, but it was exceptionally cozy, unlike our trailer, which was full of cold drafts, even with the kerosene heater working. It was never "too warm." My bedroom in the trailer got very little heat, especially with the door closed, which was why my mother used the space under my bed as a freezer.

In the process of settling in, I was passed around to several women of various ages. Lacking any similar handling by grandmothers or aunts, it surprised me that a stranger's arms could be just as familiar as my mother's. They knew about childhood fevers and had the right concoction for it. After the initial surprise of showing up at their door and taking care of my fever, everyone went back to what they were doing with no sense of urgency. There was a radio, but no TV. I saw dolls and little wheeled things scattered about along with boxes of games and puzzles, the kind of thing I didn't have because there was no room for them in the trailer.

My mother always saw to it that nothing should interfere with my bedtime prayers. Belief in a God who could save you from ruin was important to her, and she wanted it to be important to me too.

No matter where the trailer was parked, she had me repeat after her every night, *God bless Mommy and Daddy and Grandmother and Big Brother Jerry*. I knew who Mommy and Daddy were, but I'd never seen a "Grandmother," and as for "Big Brother Jerry," I had no idea who he was. He existed only in prayer and was never mentioned any other time. But prayers at bedtime are not meant to be understood. They are rituals to ease the soul to sleep, which was exactly what they did that first night I ever spent in a house.

Instead of going to the next town on the route sheet, my father had to spend the night driving back to get the trailer, but he was faced with another problem: He could not remember where he left it. There were many towns on the prairie, and they all looked the same as the morning sun blazed on a landscape of brilliant white. Was it east of Eagle Butte or west of Ridgeview? There was no lack of wisecracks and laughter as the magician, with his darkened-in eyebrows and mustache, asked in town after town—some of which he had performed in only days earlier—if anyone had seen a trailer that disappeared on the highway along with his wife and kid.

He finally got word of our whereabouts from the National Guard, who brought my mother and me by dog sled from the American Indian shack back to our home buried in a giant snow drift. With their help he extracted our four thousand pounds of yesterdays. Then we pulled it, still piled high with snow, to his next engagement. That's when I learned about another kind of house, the "doghouse," the one my father was in, and continued to be in, for the rest of their troubled marriage and beyond. During his frequent absences, my mother invited women she met in trailer park laundry rooms to see her home movies. She draped a dishtowel as a screen over the davenport and turned on the projector that gave off a peculiar electrical smell. The flickering image of a blizzard was always the main feature. The reason I remember the incident so well is because I was reminded of it so many times.

He said the reason he had to cut loose from the trailer in the first place was because it was too heavy with my mother's sweaters and furs, heels and hats, boxes of old receipts and newspapers, a sewing machine, bags of fabric and spools of every kind of thread, a projector and reels of film, photo albums, maps and postcards, everything that would serve as mileposts in my journey to find him in the snowstorm of life. He abhorred possessions as much as my mother abhorred not having them. To him, garbage cans were shrines of disposal. Perfectly good suits and shoes went in the trash for no other reason than the satisfaction of seeing them go. He read letters and threw them away all in one motion. As a devoted reader of westerns (paying no attention to authors, titles, or whether he'd read them before), they also went into the garbage. After skimming a feature on himself in the *Des Moines Register* or the *Rapid City Journal* or the *Bismarck Tribune*, it was gone too. And when he himself was gone and his ashes scattered in the ocean, my mother still bewailed the time "he left us to die in a blizzard!"

But the show went on that night in Ft. Pierre.

•••

THERE WAS A REASON why my mother clung so intensely to people and things. It might have had something to do with her own father, who evaded conscription into the Austro-Hungarian army before World War I and emigrated from Croatia to America. On May 10, 1926, Juraj Aršulić formally renounced allegiance to "Charles, Emperor of Austria and Apostolic King of Hungary," swore before God he was not an anarchist or polygamist, moved to Milwaukee, and became an American citizen under the name of George Arsulich. He married a fifteen-year-old mail-order bride from Varoš named Jelka ("Christmas Tree"), who'd lied about her age, saying she was seventeen. They had seven children, my mother the oldest.

Like many people from the ethnically mixed Balkans, her father spoke half a dozen languages and could talk to skeptical immigrants in their native Bulgarian, Slovene, Albanian, or Montenegrin, and get them to dig up cans of cash buried in the backyard and give it to him on the assurance he would invest it wisely and make them rich. With their shoveled-up tender, he leveraged his way into the ownership of numerous rental properties. In today's dollars he became a millionaire. When the stock market crashed in 1929, he lost everything. He fled Milwaukee with a "German ballerina" and a suitcase full of "concealed assets," leaving his penniless family in a soon-to-be-foreclosed-upon mansion. They lived in poverty for the rest of the Great Depression. Her father, as well as her comfortable life and possessions, had vanished. After that, whatever she acquired she held onto like survivors of starvation who hoard food.

In the 1930s, my mother appeared in several space-filling photos in the *Milwaukee Journal*, posing in rags for Hobo Days at Shorewood High, then later demonstrating the proper way to set down an electric iron so as not to start a fire, and after that she was the anonymous figure near an ice jam along Lake Michigan. She was featured for her roles in community theater, presenting a bewitching, gypsy-eyed look that drew attention away from everywhere else on the page.

While playing Princess Beatrice in Ferenc Molnár's *The Swan*, a real-life prince entered her life in the form of a slender, well-dressed man who happened to be lurking through Estabrook Park one afternoon. He'd come upon a group of young women playing softball. One of them was the extroverted actress with a propensity to immerse herself in whatever was before her. She was first to notice and then claim the impeccably dressed stranger with the pencil-thin mustache. He didn't have much to say, but was good at posing with a shiny half-dollar dancing over the back of his fingers. What Princess Barbara did not know was that her slick prince was, like her own father, missing from a family. He had a son named Jerry now old enough to ask, "When is daddy coming home?" She had unwittingly become a version of her father's "German ballerina."

•••

MY FATHER AND I COULD not have been more opposite, something he pointed out, and not by way of a compliment, when he said, "He takes after his mother." I cooked because she taught me. I read poetry, something he regarded as effeminate, but that influence came not from her but from a junior high teacher for whom I was a problem student. My mother was too flighty and unfocused to understand more than filler verse in *Reader's Digest*. Like her, I laughed easily, maybe too easily. In fact, I am one of those people prone to laughing alone as a result of something that would make no sense if spoken. Sometimes this draws unwanted attention in public, especially if it comes on suddenly. My father regarded this trait as a lack of self-control. He caused hysterics in others, picking pockets and getting women to scream in surprise, but I never saw him crack up over anything. He couldn't understand why I burst out in unexplained laughter any more than I could understand why he didn't. In the end, I think he sensed a tendency, inherited from my mother, to pry, and so he took preemptive steps to seal himself within the walls of paradox.

But we had similar qualities too. We were both loners and stingy with our words and money. We were attracted to risk and dangerous people. We were comfortable with privation. I could never confide in him because it was assumed that the mention of anything personal would upset some hidden arrangement within him that was necessary for going on stage. Over the years I bungled my way into many flagrant embarrassments that made me completely transparent to him, but he remained opaque.

There is an imbalance, probably typical of all fathers and sons, a fact of life that becomes apparent when sons have sons of their own. But I never had sons of my own. Or daughters. I had no siblings, except for my half-brother Jerry, sixteen years older than me, the unfortunate Lieutenant Colonel whom I had met only once for a few hours in a trailer park. As my father would tell me many years later, "Someday he will be your only living relative." That never happened. Instead Jerry continues to hover in the same state of quasi-existence as when he was alive.

There were only me and my parents and a compulsive quality that originated from being cooped up in a car and seeing only the back of his head. I knew every wave of his hair from behind, the arch of his ears, the stubble on his jaw—but nothing of what was beneath. I wanted to know what was in that head, partly because it was there and hidden, and partly because I had nothing else to do. Sitting in cramped quarters for days at a time, I played with pencils and paper out of monotony. I made up whole phonebooks of names—Mr. Shaw, Mr. Prawn, Stanhope, Penker, Hurdstone, etc.—that still crowd into my head like static I can't tune out. My lips and tongue move, but unless you look closely and catch me doing it, you'll never know I have this affliction. My wife sometimes hears these whispers and calls my attention to them. They stop for a while then start up again. It's comforting to know that others have this disorder too. Wayne Roland, a successful ventriloquist from Chicago, compulsively talked in imaginary voices. He did it alone as well as in the presence of others. He threw those voices into glasses and purses, a social behavior everyone had to put up with. In hotel lobbies I used to see the impressionist Wes Harrison sitting all by himself making the sound of electronic beeps, creaking doors, and whinnying horses. No one went near him. Nor did they know how well-paying his craft, or condition, whatever it might be called, proved to be.

•••

WHEN I WAS A TEENAGER, after my parents were divorced, I traveled with my father on his tours. Of course, I missed a lot of school, but learned other things instead. By that time I sat in the passenger seat next to him. Occasionally he broke the long silences with cryptic stories of when he helped his father, a contractor in Rockport, move houses by rolling them on logs and pulling them with a team of mules. "We had to be mindful of constantly dragging the last logs around to the front or the house would run aground." During the next fifty miles of silence he let these words settle into allegory. *Run aground. Look ahead. Don't trap yourself.* All those times he brought me and my mother into old hotels late at night, no matter how exhausted he was, he always walked around to make sure he knew the fire escapes. Only then did he climb into bed. I do the same in similar tinderboxes before I go to sleep, remembering his story of how Siegfried the Cannonball Juggler burned to death in the Canfield Hotel in Dubuque because he couldn't find his way out.

After another long silence he'd tell me about the time he and his older sister were on a train. The number of foods he ate did not go beyond a single digit, and one of them was bananas. He secretly bought one at a depot stop and didn't share it. When he returned to his seat, she said, "There's banana on your lip." Another long silence as this example of shame spread between us like a widening stain. Did he mean, don't be selfish? Be careful of what you desire? Don't be secretive? Don't get *caught*? The most cryptic one of all was, "I can't give you advice on women because I don't have any." Why couldn't he give me advice on women? I never thought it was because he didn't have any, but that what he had he couldn't tell me. As close as he got was telling me of the time he walked into a light post in downtown Milwaukee because he turned to look at a woman passing on the sidewalk. In the Zen-like silence that followed I pondered the depths of this too. I understood it then as I understand it now: watch out for what lures. When it came to the facts of life all he ever told me, always on my way out the door, was, "Keep your nose clean." For a long time, I never knew what that was supposed to mean.

But I would.

•••

MY FATHER'S PARENTS WERE borderline illiterates from the Ohio River town of Rockport. They raised eight children, seven of whom were high achievers. The oldest son went to West Point and became a brigadier general, serving as one of Paton's artillery marshals in World War II. The youngest son was author of *Fundamental Accounting Principles* (1955), a textbook that would earn him a thousand dollars a day in royalties. There was the dentist for the State Department who treated Eskimos in Alaska, the sister with a degree in philosophy who married the town doctor, and another daughter who was a researcher for the *Dictionary of American Regional English* (1985).

Then there was my left-handed father, John Paul, who never excelled in school or won awards like his bookish siblings. His greatest accomplishment was shooting pool with either hand. His hard-shell Baptist father, the one who moved entire houses with mules and brute force, said from under his handlebar mustache, "There's nothing in life more useless than a good pool player." His son the crack shot swaggered around Rockport as a "gay blade," in the words of his niece, my source for what little personal information I would find about his early life. Dressed like the riverboat gamblers he so greatly admired, he cruised nearby towns like Richland, Henderson, Evansville, and the tiny village of Santa Claus (known for the manufacture of decorative sleighs), looking for girls to impress. When the bowlegged peacock presented himself along the docks of Owensboro with pomaded hair and fine haberdashery, he made quite the impression on a teenage "beauty operator" who was besotted with the bad boy from the other side of the river.

One night, according to his niece, they had a lover's quarrel on the banks of the Ohio. The beautician ran up a path to higher ground, intending to leave him forever, but she remembered his dark moods and feared he might jump in the current, dapper spats and all. As Auden once said, "the only possible place for the romantic is under the waters." There was a moment when she wavered. She told my cousin later in life, "I should never have gone back." But that would have changed the destinies of several people, and there might not have been a Master of Deception, a Big Brother Jerry, or an obsessive son looking into the why of it all.

•••

IN HIS FIFTIES MY father met a woman named Jane in a Chicago park under circumstances not unlike those he met my mother. They never married, but she did accompany him around the country for twenty years, longer than my mother. The stage life of "the lovely assistant" lasts as long as that of a burlesque dancer or contortionist, which is roughly the duration of the reproductive years. Jane came along too late to replace my mother's alluring role, yet in middle age she still had much of her youthful looks, as did my mother. My father aged into white-haired magnificence, his smile still beaming with the teeth of a Cheshire cat. That is, when he chose to show them, which was seldom in private, especially after what happened years later to my Big Brother Jerry.

Whether it was Chicago, Phoenix, or Tampa, he and Jane lived separately. As far as I know, they never slept in the same bed nor openly showed affection. No hugging, no kissing, no handholding. But I wasn't with them all that time, so who knows what I might have missed? From what I could see, their relationship was one of droll acceptance. She talked compulsively; he ignored her. When they lived in Chicago she went on errands, leaving her car unlocked, the keys in the ignition, and her purse on the seat next to her aggressively territorial Doberman. She took only enough money to buy what she needed and left the rest in her purse, where it could not have been safer. The dog shared her bed, and under her pillow she kept a gun. "You're a tough old broad," he liked to say whenever he could get a word in, and this always made her smile.

She worked as a bookkeeper and excelled at managing other people's funds, but not her own, a family trait passed down to her daughter, one of the original Playboy Bunnies, and to her granddaughter, who also found herself in frequent difficulties financial and otherwise. Whichever of them happened to be in trouble at the moment, one or the other came in to help. The Playboy Bunny lived with her husband on a horse ranch in the Chicago suburbs. After he was injured in a riding accident, he died in the hospital under suspicious circumstances. Coffee grounds were reportedly found in his bloodstream. The Bunny sued the hospital and from what I heard it went bankrupt. While working at the Playboy resort in Lake Geneva, Wisconsin, she married again, this time to the resort's stable operator. They moved to Phoenix, where he legally changed his name to Black Bart and hired himself out at parades and festivals as a professional cowboy on a white horse. My father described him as a "blowhard," but Black Bart seemed cordial enough to me the one time he took me riding at the Pointe Hilton Resort.

According to the *Arizona Republic*, the Bunny forged Black Bart's signature on a $160,000 life insurance policy, then hired a hit man for $25,000 to ambush him on his doorstep and put a bullet between his eyes with a silencer-equipped pistol. She was found guilty of first-degree murder and sentenced to life in prison. As an example of how secretive things were with Jane and my father, it took almost five years for me to find out about the incident from the Bunny's granddaughter, who had moved to Tampa to help Jane when my father took ill. All she said was, "They think my mom did it." By then my father was in a medical bed in Jane's living room coughing mucus day and night, filling up shopping bags with tissues. Thirty years earlier he quit a four-pack-a-day smoking habit cold turkey, but lung cancer got him anyway.

As his health worsened, Jane became frustrated. Droll acceptance gave way to coldness. She refused to wash his hair, shave him, or cut his toenails—things I helped him with myself on weekly flights to Tampa from Minneapolis. Toward the end, oatmeal was all he could eat. I saw her once plunk down a bowl in front of him and walk away in disgust, as his eyes followed her.

The last I talked to him was by pay phone from a rest area on a North Dakota freeway. He anxiously tried to tell me something but was strangely incoherent. In frustration I had him put Jane back on. She talked faster than usual, and I didn't get a chance to ask her why he was acting so different. A few days later her granddaughter left a message on my answering machine saying that he had died. When I called Jane, she made a point of saying she was the only one present as he passed away peacefully with a deck of cards in his hand. There was no autopsy. She had him immediately cremated and arranged for the Neptune Society to scatter his ashes in the Gulf of Mexico.

After that, she moved to a different house where she had a stroke and was in a medical bed herself. Her granddaughter moved back in to help out. When I flew down to visit her, she was just as garrulous, except every fourth or fifth word was the wrong one. Her granddaughter told me her memory was slipping. Propped up on a shelf at the foot of her bed was an unframed publicity photo of my father in his younger days, smiling broadly in the suit of tails he wore on stage.

"Why did you put that photo there?" Jane asked her grand-daughter. "Because Jackie's here?"

"It's been there all the time, Grandma."

"No, it hasn't. You just put it there this morning." I noticed the eight-by-ten glossy had not yet curled from the humidity.

That was the last I saw her. I wrote her several letters after that, but she didn't answer them. The last one was returned rubber-stamped "UNKNOWN."

After my father's withdrawal from worldly existence, he entered the realm of dream, appearing and disappearing as frequently as when he was alive, arriving from somewhere before departing for somewhere else. As in real life, I am elated to see him return, his ghostly form carrying a wardrobe bag. I always say something like, "It's been so long..." He says nothing. Or, instead of arriving, he departs for an unknown stage with the same wardrobe bag, and no indication of when he will return. In these dreams, if he smiles at all, it's his stage smile, projecting everything but revealing nothing. Even in the Underworld, he remains the Master of Deception.

•••

I SUPPOSE IT SHOULD not be surprising that in some way we all want to *be* the people we admire. We copy the fashions of pop stars and imitate sports heroes. I don't know how often sons want to be their fathers. They are more likely to want the opposite, and then become their fathers anyway. Adults asked me all the time if I was going to follow "in dad's footsteps," and I always said no, I did not want to be a magician. Although my father didn't follow his father's footsteps either, he spent his life moving stuff by sheer will, mostly his physical self. My great model in life was the Prince of Pantomime, Billy Papon. Of all the people we encountered in places with names I would never remember, he was the one I most wanted to be. And in some respects, I might even say that I did eventually become him.

According to his publicity brochure, he could "reproduce practically any sound for six to twenty-five minutes, depending on the amount of time you want." In twenty-four-point type it proclaimed he did "Nothing Obscene" and was a "Good Clean all-around Entertainer." He imitated a locomotive and the sound of a saw cutting down a tree. With my mind prone to endless repetition I mimicked his mimicry beyond my parents' tolerance. He played "Peg o' My Heart" on a huge harmonica, then on progressively smaller ones, ending with one hardly bigger than a finger joint that he played without using his hands. Then he swallowed it. Or pretended to. The pantomime part of his act consisted of lip-syncing "The Old Sow Song" from a record player off stage, complete with squeals and snorts. That always went over well. Then came my favorite, his pantomime of an aria from *The Barber of Seville* while shaking his hair down over his face in a populist parody of high art. He had a clever way of combing it to disguise its unusual length, leading to the surprise when it fell over his face.

"I keep telling barbers to cut the sides but leave the top long," I'd heard him say. "I'm in show business and need my hair a certain way for a skit. When they see me pull a strand of hair down to my chin to show them how it should be, it goes against everything they know about cutting hair. I have to watch them, especially the old timers, because their fingers can't help themselves and they cut it short anyway."

When I was a teenager, I told barbers the same thing. I understood what he meant about barbers getting snip-happy and cutting it short anyway. In Billy's case it was part of his routine, but in my case, it made no sense to anyone but me. I still tell hair stylists to "keep it longer on top," but not so long that I can shake it over my eyes for attention like I used to.

After his part in the floor show I followed him like a fly out to his car, where he packed his battered record player and harmonicas in the trunk next to boxes of what he said were dinosaur eggs. I was just as fascinated by them as he was. From then on I collected any ovoid rock that resembled the ones in his trunk. My father had to find a place to stow this unnecessary poundage in an already overloaded car and trailer. He tried throwing a few away when I wasn't looking, but I had plenty of time to pore over and memorize every detail of their surface, and I knew immediately which ones were gone. Carrying rocks around in the trailer reached such a limit that he sent one of the eggs Billy gave me to the geology department at the University of Kansas for analysis. He showed me their letter on official stationery that stated the sample was not a dinosaur egg but a "sedimentary accretion." He hoped this would discourage me and hopefully shift my interest to feathers or leaves, or better yet sand grains, but it did not. I expanded my hunts for other types of fossils and filled boxes with brachiopods from gravel side roads, bivalves from eroded areas outside trailer parks, and ammonoids from creek beds. I picked up taconite pellets, volcanic gabbros, agates, crystals, and geodes. I still can't walk over any loose aggregate without looking down. Recently I found a perfect Rafinesquina brachiopod that had made its way from the bottom of a 450-million-year-old sea to the butt-littered side door of a Quality Inn in Redwood Falls, Minnesota. Its two perfectly preserved perforations at the hinge have impressed no one, but if the Prince of Pantomime were alive today, he would be just as excited about the find as I am.

At night, instead of looking down for dinosaur eggs, the Prince of Pantomime looked up at the stars. He knew the names of ones you could barely see and the constellations they were in. I learned from him that Worcestershire sauce could go on ice cream, and if you turned a piece of toast and jelly upside down, you couldn't taste the jelly. I tried it and still tasted the jelly, but that did not make me doubt the infallibility of this man who was the first genius I ever met.

•••

I WAS SURROUNDED BY lies and exaggerations that were regarded as perfectly legitimate and necessary. They were not compulsive lies but lies of utility. Billy once visited the Grand Ole Opry in Nashville and henceforth advertised himself as "seen at the Grand Ole Opry!" My father performed on a stage where Frank Sinatra appeared several years earlier, so he claimed he "shared the stage with Frank Sinatra!" The truth was that he *did* appear with famous people, but less prestigious ones like Clarabell the Clown from the *Howdy Doody Show.* It was at an outdoor fair with the audience crowding around the stage. My mother was as dazzled by Clarabell as though he were Frank Sinatra and captured the clown in action with her 3-D StereoRealist camera. I still have the slide, which has to be seen through a viewer. In the hyper-reality of three dimensions, Clarabell appears clearer and more distinct than he ever did in his fuzzy black-and-white image on TV. In the 3-D color slide every flaw of his flimsy clown suit is visible, as well as the nicked prop box and battered horn attached to his waist. My father had no acting ability outside his role of Master of Deception, so playing straight man in Clarabell's lame, horn-honking spoof came off wooden and flat. It didn't matter, though. All anyone cared about was seeing Clarabell, *live from TV!* A rough-looking man with tattooed arms who looked like a sunbaked carnie acted as chaperone to keep the kids back. Kiddy show personalities knew that TV turned them into something kids wanted to grab. Clarabell, Gabby Hayes, Hopalong Cassidy, or Mr. Toot could not step out of character and yell, "Get back!!" so they had to have handlers to do it for them. Sometimes I had to act as my father's handler, keeping little hands off the birds, his props—or him. Even though I was a kid myself, I knew that kids in audiences had no awareness of what monsters they could be if given the chance. It was one of the reasons I decided not to have any of my own—a choice I have never regretted.

•••

IN SOME WAYS MY life wasn't that much different from other children. I had chores, like using a snow shovel to scoop away mayflies that piled up on the footlights at outdoor shows in river towns. If that wasn't done, the stage would slowly go dark. Whether it was a nightclub, a county fair, or a hotel banquet, one assignment was always the same: repack my father's props in a meticulously precise order, folding silks, stacking dove bags, and breaking down the so-called "Box Trick" (also known as "Metamorphosis," "Sub Trunk," or "Houdini Trunk Escape") where my father locked my mother in a trunk and then instantly switched places with her. It wasn't easy moving something that heavy up and down stairs and pushing doors open against the wind, but it built up my strength so I could hold my own if I had to on a hostile playground.

There were strict rules I had to follow, like never touch or even show an interest in another performer's props. It would have been worse than touching or handling a stranger's baby without permission, or a woman's purse. Glittery balance balls, puppets, and juggler's hoops were colorful and alluring, and in the spotlight were the mystical and untouchable reality of the spectacle. This was especially true for ventriloquist dummies, with their uncanny, fixed expressions. Since nonperformers knew nothing of the touch taboo, part of my duty was to make sure, like a museum guard, they kept their hands to themselves. But they touched anyway. One time I came upon several people who took it upon themselves to inspect the inside of Louie, one of Grover Ruwe's ventriloquist dummies, and gloat over the mechanisms on the stick. It would have been no different than putting their hands down his pants.

"Hey, whatta ya doing?" said Ruwe when he caught them.

"It's funny to see how it works…"

"Yeah, well."

They would have had to probe much deeper to see the real inside of Louie, the "brain" clandestinely sealed in the dummy's head, a crude clockwork of cords, levers, and swivels unrecognizable as anything human. As he put his dummy away, I knew, if no one else did, that a grave sin had been committed.

Another time I caught a group inspecting the lid to my father's Trunk Escape. They found the trap door, which even I had never seen. The trespassers absorbed themselves in morbid gawking. When my father arrived and caught them, he looked helpless and hurt. "It's still a good trick," a woman said, but my father's silence indicated that what they had done could not be undone.

Trained animals were also considered props, and interaction with them was especially forbidden. They existed for just one purpose: to work. Not to pet, not to talk to, not even to look at. They traveled like I did, in restricted quarters and with specific duties, except with no freedom to wander about. Every aspect of their lives was carefully regulated. I saw chimpanzees in little tuxes and tutus reach out their arms to me plaintively as they passed, but I'd been told that although they were well-trained, they could take a mouthful out of my face and that would interfere with show time.

The ultimate taboo was having anything to do with a performing child. No talking with, no standing next to. No being in the same *room* with. We arrived at a county fair in some town in Texas where, in the infield behind the grandstand stage, I saw a metal tower held up with guy wires. I recognized it as a sway pole, a metal pipe that twangs from side to side in a wide arc with a person or persons clutched at the top. They had a tendency to weaken and break, like bending a coat hanger back and forth. The death rate for sway pole acts was said to be one hundred percent and some towns banned them altogether by city ordinance, usually after a horrible accident. Fiberglass eventually replaced metal poles, but some aerialists still used the old ones because they did not want to change what was familiar.

When the spotlight was directed to their perch high up in the stars, all backstage activity stopped. Other performers came out of dressing tents with makeup half removed to look up and see them so far above the stage as if to transcend it altogether. There was hardly a need for high acts to even be backstage since they performed above and beyond it. The scarcity of their presence only added to their mystique among the other performers. If you happened to see them up close you might not recognize their faces. They were usually much older and less glamorous than you expected. The ones we worked with were often from other countries, refugees who had performed throughout the War, staying alive by keeping one step ahead of invading armies sometimes close enough to be seen in the distance from their elevated perches. Like human spiders they anchored guy wires and turnbuckles in every conceivable place and made a living defying death against a backdrop of death. Besides being nationally ambiguous, they were unconstrained by boundaries both horizontal and vertical.

"They're from Mongolia," my father said. "A mother and daughter. The girl isn't much older than you are. Their trailer is parked back in the infield. I want you to understand that under no circumstances are you to go over there. Do not play with the girl."

"What if she comes over here?"

"You say hello, but that's all."

"But what if she wants to play with me?"

"Just say you have to help with props or something. Then get away from her and stay away."

The strength and coordination of performing children could not in any way be compromised. Distraction from an off-stage squabble could be just enough to cause a mishap. They could not afford to fall and hurt themselves while running around. Focus had to be on one thing and nothing else, because their family's survival depended on it.

Up in the sky, the Mongolian mother-daughter looked like two graceful young women, but up close the age difference was obvious. The next afternoon the girl, whose name was Sonya, carried a pail to get water from a faucet somewhere on the midway. She said hi to me and, following my father's rule, I said hi back but no more. I wondered if that might have been the only word she had spoken to another child in weeks.

I saw her again in the empty band pavilion next to the stage, this time paging through a scrapbook of pictures cut out of magazines. My curiosity overrode all prohibitions, so I went over to see what she was doing.

"This is the daddy," she said, pointing to a stereotypical daddy's face at the bottom of the page. If she spoke in a foreign language, I don't remember it. "He went away, and mommy says he's never coming back. This is the mommy." At the precarious top of the page was a woman in an evening dress smiling blissfully as she stood before a stove. "And these are all the children." She had pasted down running, jumping children with their dogs and bikes. Each had a detailed imaginary past.

"These two are brother and sister, and this girl in the yellow dress is an orphan. The dog's name is Trixie, and she belongs to the boy on the bicycle. This is the man who makes candy for all the people who live in the castle, but only this girl knows how to get there, and one night she got lost in the woods…"

Every page revealed new people, children, and animals, new paths, grottos, and castles with kings and queens and wizards and angels. She solved the problem of not knowing any real people by inventing her own. Isolation will do that. After allowing myself to be lured by her imaginary world, I remembered my father's warning. Abruptly I said, "I have to help with some props." There was no goodbye, just like there was no hello. I went back to the bandshell later to see if she might still be there, but she was gone. I never saw her again except high above the ground.

Falling, of course, is always an occupational hazard of high acts. They all thought it would never happen to them, but of course it did. If it were a family of performers, and one or more of them fell, the survivors would be up on the rigging for the next performance. It was a doctrine of commitment that went back centuries. Some were known to plunge to the ground and live, only to go back up on the rigging when they recovered. The most dangerous aspect of what they did was the part that no one saw: setting up and taking down the equipment. When the engagement was over, Sonya's mother took down their sway pole with labor provided by the fair, but only her and Sonya went up on the strutting. Long after midnight, their car and trailer loaded with the disassembled defiance of death, they drove off to the next fairgrounds.

I heard some time later that Sonya's mother fell to her death— not during a performance, but while taking down the rigging. They said it wasn't a long drop, but it does not have to be. Aerialists were known to survive a fifty-foot plunge but die falling down the stairs or tripping on a sidewalk crack. I never knew what happened to Sonya. They said she didn't have any other relatives so maybe she was sent back to Mongolia or became a ward of the state and went to an orphanage. Or maybe she was adopted by a local family and grew up as a farm wife—perhaps even a happy one. If she's alive, maybe she remembers me. Maybe not. I don't know the town where our interlude in the bandshell took place, nor where or when her mother died. It seems unlikely she will ever read these words, but I still carry the burden of wondering whether I might have upset some profound balance that resulted in her mother joining the imaginary daddy in her scrap book who was also never coming back.

MEET THE NEIGHBORS

MY FATHER LEFT HIS trace on the pamphlets and local maps my mother picked up (and kept forever), with calculations and recalculations of how long it would take to get to a nightclub called the Rio Rosa in Mexico City. Because she insisted on taking the side roads, he often had to detach the trailer and have it ferried across rivers without bridges. It rocked dangerously back and forth on crude barges while shirtless men waded out in the water and pulled it by hand with ropes. One wrong jostle and our home and all the evidence on which these pages are based would have been swept away downstream. At one crossing our car was surrounded by a group of kids who looked in the open windows, and when they saw the rabbit and birds in the back seat, they reached in from all sides to try and touch them. Sunglasses disappeared, then a cigarette lighter, then a roll of film. To distract everyone away from the car, my father put on his stage smile and pulled a few centavos out of the air and gave them away, but that only swelled the crowd to include practically every man, woman, and child within walking distance. Word spread so fast that when he arrived on the other side of the river a crowd had already gathered to see the smiling gringo who could pull money out of the air and give it away.

"They've never seen a trailer before," said my mother, squinting through the lens of her eight-millimeter camera filming what was happening. "Let them have a look inside. That should be interesting."

"I don't think you want to do that," my father said. "Not here."

She stopped to rewind the camera so it could shoot another ten seconds. "Oh, go ahead. What can happen?"

He opened the door and everyone rushed to peer inside this strange house on wheels. Traveling over unpaved roads shook the cabinet doors open and the contents had fallen out onto the floor. Arms snaked in from all directions snatching a measuring cup here, a box of tapioca there. Before the ten-second windup time was over, several kids had pushed their way inside and it took some doing to get them out.

The Rio Rosa, a place the tourist booklet, *El Mirón* (*The Gazer*), advised "not to visit without the escort of a reliable guide." Working through a not-so-competent translator, my father warmed up the crowds for Brazilian banjoist José da Silva ("the man with the sticky fingers") and the "songs and gayness of Oscar Laplana." I sat in the dressing room with my body wedged between female flamenco dancers with cascades of hair and endless ruffles enveloping me in body heat and perfume while they waited for their dance numbers.

We stayed at one of the cheaper trailer parks for a couple of pesos a night among a few barely road-worthy pre-war models. The washroom was a shack with a laundry tub and hand-cranked wringer. The showers were fenced off into men's and women's with cold water only, and the drains were teeming with palmetto bugs. There was an open cesspool for emptying "the bucket," since bathrooms in trailers, even newer models, were not yet standard. Trailer parks were often situated near garbage dumps, but in this case the park *was* the dump. We parked next to a massive pile of trash that was supposed to have been burned in several oil drums but the job had been put off until a tomorrow that never came. Piles of food scraps and fruit rinds were alive with flies, and the sandy ground was mixed with every color of broken glass that glittered in the sun. Wind blew paper up against the sides of the trailer like a snow drift.

I made friends with a boy who spent his time picking through the garbage. I'll call him Javier, though I don't know if I ever knew his name at all. His shirt and pants were too big, and his left and right sock and shoe were all mismatched. His dark, unwashed skin was covered with a powdering of dust, and he smelled like a trash can when you lift the lid. He did not live in the trailer park, just foraged in the dump there. The pack of friends he ran with welcomed me to join them. Here I did not have to stand at a safe distance as I often did in America until I was sure the kids were friendly. Having a playmate at all was a blessing, and here I had more than I could count. When they weren't digging in the garbage, they swung on an old tire hung from a frayed rope or climbed on a fallen, sun-bleached tree that functioned as a jungle gym. None of them spoke English, but I don't remember that being a problem as they showed me how to scavenge discarded boxes of detergent, where a surprising amount remained stuck in the bottom corners. Honey jars could be turned upside down and the residue collected. Thrown-away socks could be mended. Who said they had to match? They collected soap slivers, which could be melted down into fresh bars. I had to watch out for standing in certain places where ants would swarm up my legs and bite me with stinging pincers. Javier generously shared a half-empty bag of peanuts he found buried along with a package of hardened marshmallows that tasted all the more delicious for having been gleaned from a fly-buzzing heap. When my mother looked out the trailer window and saw what I was doing, she called me inside for a lecture on germs. After that, Javier and I dug around on the other side of the pile where she couldn't see us.

While she slept late in the morning (as was her custom), my father and I (as was our custom) took a long walk. It was one of the few times I had his attention all to myself.

"Watch out for the ant hills," I warned him. "They'll climb up your legs and bite you."

We squatted down to watch them going about their business.

"They carry sand up one grain at a time," he said. "There has to be a first grain, then a second grain, and so forth, until there's a hill. One grain of sand doesn't make a hill, nor does two or even ten. But at some point, there's a hill. How many would that be?"

"A hundred?"

"A hundred grains of sand isn't very much. But let's say a hundred grains of sand makes a hill. Take away one grain. Is it still a hill? Or take away two or ten. At what point is it not a hill?"

"Like a pile of garbage."

"Exactly. How many pieces of garbage do you have to take away before it's no longer a pile of garbage? One thing you can't take away from garbage, even if it's down to just one piece, and that's germs. Good reason why you shouldn't be in it. So, listen to your mother."

She decided that one way to keep me away from Javier and his garbage-picking friends was to go out sightseeing. Since my father's performances were at night, the days were free for us to go around and look at everything that caught her attention in nearby villages. She filmed *campesinos* setting up market stalls, women carrying laundry on their heads, donkeys piled high with firewood, and my father in a sombrero she'd made him wear even though he looked ridiculous wearing it. She brought us to jai alai matches, cathedrals, and mariachi parades. "Isn't this wonderful?" she said. "We have to see a bullfight before we leave."

My father once told me he didn't like fishing because he was afraid he'd hurt the fish, so watching a bull stabbed to death for sport was beyond his tolerance.

But my mother persisted.

"All right," he said with great reluctance. "I'll take you to your bullfight."

At the arena a huge crowd watched gaudily dressed matadors and picadors on horses enter to the music of majesty and pomp. Then a frisky bull was released and the crowd cheered. They continued cheering as a matador thrust spears into its withers until blood ran down its black fur. They cheered in waves as the creature, drenched in red, charged the matador's cape. After the final ritualized sword thrust, a stream of blood ran out of its nose and mouth before it fell over dead.

"That was the most revolting thing I have ever seen," he said from under his sombrero on our way out.

"Oh, come on," my mother said. "It's cultural."

•••

AFTER HIS LAST PERFORMANCE at the Rio Rosa we had to leave Mexico in a hurry because in two days he was due at an Air Force base in Rapid City. It would be another nonstop drive, this one about the same distance as to the coast of Africa. As we pulled out of the trailer park in the middle of the night, we dragged an accumulation of windblown garbage that took miles to dislodge. Tourist brochures warned people not to travel the mountain roads at night, certainly not with an overloaded trailer, but my father was not a tourist, nor did he have a choice. With our trailer home behind us, we pushed on through the Sierras, interrupted by sudden stops as headlights came around blind mountain curves. I slept in the back seat dreaming of anthills and marshmallows.

The Interstate Commerce Commission (ICC) limited truckers' time on the road to no more than ten hours in a single day and no more than sixty hours total for the week. Floor show acts were not regulated by the ICC, and they greatly exceeded those limits on a regular basis. The marathon car trips of Kerouac and the beats were child's play compared to the routine travels of entertainers, who had the added constraint of appearing fresh and performing exacting stunts in wardrobe when they reached their destinations.

I often heard the story of Zabo Cantina, the Chinese hand balancer, booked on a typical jump from Los Angeles to Grand Junction, Colorado, an 800-mile drive. The agent booked him two days later in Beresford, New Brunswick, of all places, a distance of more than 2,500 miles from LA. This was before freeways and cruise control. Since agents always distorted distance on the short side, Zabo was probably told, "By the time you get to Grand Junction you're almost halfway there!"

He dutifully made the drive, first to Grand Junction, then left immediately the same night for New Brunswick. Into the second day he began to empty bagged ice inside his clothes to stay awake. When he arrived in Beresford he'd been on the road continuously for fifty hours, and so the story went, was hallucinating from lack of sleep. His clothes were soaked with melted ice and he didn't look like a hand balancer at all but a sweating drunk who had wet his pants. The client tried to cancel his appearance, which meant that Zabo wouldn't get paid, but he was rational enough to produce a legally binding contract and insist that it be honored. He changed into his stage wardrobe and when his time came in the lineup, he did sixteen minutes on his hands. For all the years this tale circulated, it was said that Zabo, like any seasoned performer, was so skilled at what he did that he balanced on blocks, canes, and chairs, and did all the difficult one-hand stands, tiger bends, planches, and V-sits *while sound asleep.*

Afterward, according to my father, he changed back into his wet clothes, got in his car, and drove almost a thousand feet before passing out for ten hours. When he woke up, he continued back to LA—nonstop—with a net profit of fifty dollars. "In those days," my father said, "that was a lot of money."

To keep his slender body as light as possible Zabo never ate anything more than clear soup and tea. With that kind of self-discipline, he could have eaten for months on fifty dollars. The careers of hand balancers have a brief shelf-life. Whatever they make from their act has to be made before they hit forty at the oldest, although there are always exceptions (like Jose Colé, who did the gaffed one finger handstand into his fifties). Zabo, like all variety acts, was motivated to secure every possible engagement no matter how far he had to travel.

The limits of sleep deprivation were hardly known until the late 1950s, when a New York disk jockey stayed awake for eight days as a publicity stunt. They finally put him to bed when he started hallucinating bugs and mice. Then a San Diego teenager pushed himself to stay awake for eleven days until his whole sense of reality caved in. A British woman reportedly stayed awake for almost nineteen days while competing in a marathon rocking-chair contest. The record has steadily been broken ever since. So driving one, two, or even three days without sleep was well within the known human limits.

Operating a car after prolonged lack of sleep puts a person into what experts call "vigilance decrement." Driving under those conditions drops to the level of automatism with periods of mini-sleep blackouts. Steering wheel movements increase from the one to five-degree range to a six to ten-degree range, most suitable for fishtailing a trailer over a canyon wall. In the last moment of consciousness before hitting the canyon floor, the autonomic nervous system will gush so much adrenaline you will be more awake than ever before and a panoramic autobiography will flash through your mind in the instant before your head is crushed. Even though every moment on the road was a danger, especially those times when my father slammed on the brakes and I could feel the massive momentum of our home pushing us from behind, I still felt safe in his hands.

For my father, being a magician was a battle for wakefulness with potentially disastrous consequences, and to be a magician's son was to rock back and forth in the back seat in the endless throes of ceaseless perseverance. When we finally arrived at Ellsworth Air Force base, he had been driving continuously for forty-eight hours. My mother got out of the car and had trouble keeping her balance. I was mumbling some repetitive nonsense and longing for the chance to run anywhere—even in circles, if I had to. In the extreme stages of fatigue, complaining of speckles in front of his eyes, my father put on his suit of tails with a fresh cardboard front and took the stage at the Officer's Club that night, where he pulled cards out of the air for lieutenants, colonels, and majors, and their wives, with a smile framed by the lines of a perfect mustache.

•••

FOR THREE WEEKS WE stayed at a trailer park in Rapid City waiting for Harvester Show season to begin. The cold autumn winds blew tumbleweeds, newspapers, and cardboard up against the trailer. Roosting in the same park for the same reason were several people we knew, including Larry Thompson ("America's Foremost Juggler") and his wife Bobbi, and Tom Gary ("Comedy a la Mode") and his wife Jeanne. In these longer intervals between shows my father retreated into the trailer, filled with smoke from his Chesterfields, and sat with a bug-eyed stare, whiskers growing out, mutating into a frightening presence. He lost himself in thoughts of an apparently tortuous nature while his right hand went through endless repetitive motions until the cards he was handling showed enough wear they had to be thrown away. He knew how to be suave as the occasion required, but if there was no occasion, there was nothing to be suave for.

The only time he went out was in the morning to walk with me through nearby gullies and waste areas. "Watch this," I'd say, then balance on something, jump over something, or throw something to make it plop or splash.

"Very good. We'll make you next-to-closing act."

There could be no higher praise.

The usual morning chore among those in trailers without bathrooms (which was most of them) was to carry "the bucket" to empty in the washroom toilet. In one of these processions I met a boy named Josh walking with his mother. We became instant playmates. Kids were technically not supposed to be in the ruin and sludge surrounding most trailer parks because it was dangerous. But the more adventurous ones, like me and Josh, went there anyway. He was already familiar with the area and showed me an abandoned machine shop consisting of a concrete foundation, four partial walls, and piles of debris and metal parts. We ignored the "KEEP OUT" sign and went inside where we found a pit filled with dark, oily liquid partially covered by corrugated metal sheets.

"Watch out for the rusted parts," he said. "You could trip and fall in. Can you swim?"

"No."

"Neither can I."

Cold winds carried the smell of burning leaves mingled with the odor of grease and rotten wood as we enjoyed the thrill of bouncing up and down on the rusted metal sheets over the pit.

•••

MY MOTHER WASTED NO time presenting herself to other young mothers washing clothes in the laundry room and hanging them up on communal clotheslines while toddlers played at their feet. They were the wives of the construction workers, miners, and water tower painters so much in demand after the War. She invited them to our trailer while my father went over to visit Tom Gary or the juggler. In trying to fit in, my mother didn't say much about show business. After explaining that we weren't with the circus or the carnival, she joined their conversation on babies and the best places to buy meat.

"The hardest thing about moving into a new trailer park is finding a doctor," she said. "Our son cut his foot in some town in

Iowa and needed stitches. Just our luck it had to be on a Sunday. So, we're driving all around looking for a doctor. Finally, I found someone who opened up just for us. He was an older man and his office was full of mounted animal heads. I think he was really a taxidermist."

When the time was right, she draped a dishtowel over the back of the davenport to serve as a screen, then pulled down the shades and threaded a reel of film into the little projector. A glowing white square appeared with flickering black flecks that suddenly came alive with moving images. The laundry room mothers had traveled very little if at all, so they were amazed to see the very trailer they were sitting in rocking on a barge pulled across a river in Mexico only a few days before. There were four- and six-second shots of men riding on the haunches of burros, beggar children cavorting before the camera for a few centavos, and a man with a mustache and funny sombrero looking none too happy at the sight of a dead bull dragged by mules out of an arena.

She rewound Mexico then threaded up the blizzard.

•••

As she put down her temporary roots, trouble was already beginning. The juggler and his wife, Bobbi, who were lovebirds in public, started fighting in private. Trailers were not at all soundproof, so everyone could hear them. I was at the shower room sinks with my father one night when the juggler came in with blood all over the front of his shirt.

"I went into town to shoot a little pool and two guys wanted to play for money," he said while a couple of other men at the sinks listened too. "I said okay. We're playing, and I tell them I'm a juggler in show business and they ask if I'm with the carnival. I tell them I'm higher class than that. They start laughing so I tell them I did a show once with Eleanor Roosevelt in the audience. They start in on how she's too free with the coloreds and all that kind of crap and keep referring to me as a carnie. I lean over for a shot and one of them bumps into me and makes me miss so I put the ball back to take the shot again. They tell me I can't do that, but I line up the shot anyway and one tries to stop me. It gets a little rough at that point and one of them punches me in the nose. I'm an entertainer. I've got a better sense of timing than they do. I pick up three pool balls and start juggling just to distract them. Then I throw two balls—*pow! pow!*—and hit the bastards right in the face. Then I get the hell out of there fast."

One of the men overhearing this said, "Eleanor Roosevelt?"

The juggler ignored him.

On Sunday, Bobbi and my mother dressed up in white gloves and hats with netted veils and went to Mass as if they lived in town and belonged to the parish. My father stayed in the trailer and practiced card maneuvers, his own form of prayer. To me, church was a kind of performance with a stage and an audience but no applause. I could not put it together, this God business, but since my mother and the juggler's wife and so many others took it seriously, I had to conclude there must be something to it.

"How come you don't go to church with us?" I asked my father.

"Your grandparents went to church all the time in Rockport, not just on Sunday. They sang the hymns, and when they weren't in church, they talked about hell and God's will. It gave them comfort. But it didn't work for me. You and your mother can go. Maybe it will give you comfort someday."

In her usual assertive way, my mother brought me to the sacristy after the service to meet the priest. As he was hanging up his chasuble, I thrust out my hand and said, "Good show, Father!"

•••

AS IT NEARED THANKSGIVING, my mother and Bobbi began spending time with an elderly lady whose name I have no trouble remembering,

Mrs. Coffee, who lived alone in a long, elegant trailer with a forward-slanting front and an awning over the door. It was more spacious than any trailer I'd been in, with carpeting and shelves decorated with little saltshakers in the shape of animals. Clearly not a trailer for pulling through the mountains. It had a toilet and shower. My mother and Bobbi were delighted to be in such genteel company, but none of them could foresee the trouble ahead.

"Last year," said Mrs. Coffee, "a man stayed in the park who could pull himself through a tennis racquet. Have you ever heard of such a thing?"

"I know who you mean. It's Hal Plummer. I don't even like his name. It reminds me of plumbing, and plumbing reminds me of a toilet, something we don't have in our trailer."

We'd worked with Hal Plummer, the Human Pretzel, countless times. He was a quiet man who lived alone in a type of small trailer called a "Canned Ham" because of its shape. I'm sure he didn't have a toilet either. To open his act, they wheeled him on stage inside a closed suitcase like a piece of luggage. He pushed open the lid and unfolded himself into a standing position, then proceeded to bend over backward and look at the audience with his face between his ankles. When the Pretzel pulled his heels behind his head and walked on his hands like a crab, there was a prominent bulge where his pants gathered up between his legs. This was the part that disgusted my mother most. She saw the Human Pretzel not as an entertainer but as a repulsive eugenic mistake.

"And who, may I ask, is that man with those frightful whips?"

"That's Jean's husband," my mother said. "Tom Gary. He whips cigarettes out of his wife's mouth."

This made Mrs. Coffee gasp.

Tom Gary did what was known in the business as a "drunk act," which could not be advertised as such in Puritan America, so he was booked as "Comedy a la Mode," with pie as stand-in for booze. It consisted of swagger and sight gags. While the band played background music, his wife Jean, dressed as a cigarette girl in a ruffled skirt (it was said he won her in a poker game), put down several plates and glasses on a small table covered with a cloth. Then he took a corner in each hand and suddenly pulled it out from under the plates and glasses without disturbing them. Just as deftly, he shoved the tablecloth *back* underneath. It happened so fast that sometimes the audience didn't get it. Then he brought out the dog, a Manchester terrier. As he crooned questions, the dog was supposed to howl answers that sounded more or less like "Who?" or "Why?" Audiences sometimes didn't get that either. What really got their attention was the loud whips. His wife lit a cigarette and casually began smoking it. Without any warning he cracked it out of her mouth with an eight-foot bullwhip.

That's what passed for entertainment on those long winter nights before television.

His closing stunt was to pull a bald man out of the audience and put a dime on his head. With a terrifying crack that shook the walls he whipped off the dime. No one could see that the end of the whip cracked far to the side and then merely brushed the dime off, but once in a while he accidentally wrapped it around the stooge's head. It didn't cause any injury but definitely looked bad. If the bald man had the temerity to go back to the dressing room after the show and say, "Came a little low with that whip, don'tcha think?" Gary would pull himself up to his full man-mountain height and say, "If I'd a come low with that whip, I'd a taken yer head clean off!"

He spent his time alone in a different way than my father. Whenever Josh and I passed his trailer we heard his loud, blustery voice booming something like, "I owe Ollie!" or "Yellow owls!" followed by the howling of a dog. Every kid in the park thought he was just another guy who was crazy *because of the War*, but he was actually rehearsing his talking dog. Every day he sat down with a plate of raw meat cut into little pieces and began the session. He said things at a certain pitch that made the creature howl. If the howl sounded like a word that could be a punchline, it got a treat. But the animal was getting old and stubborn and sometimes decided to clam up in the middle of the act. It didn't matter, though, because they forgot the dog as soon as the whips came out.

My father could go through his card manipulations inside our trailer in privacy, but Tom Gary had to practice his whips outside. The loud noise attracted kids from all over the trailer park who gathered around to watch. He ignored them while he worked on snapping cigarettes out of his wife's mouth, trying not to take the skin off her nose. Boys started imitating him, making their own whips out of a stick and a length of rope. They enjoyed snapping them against the sides of trailers and cardboard boxes. Josh snapped his against garbage cans and took the seed pods off the tops of dry weeds. When a toddler waddled by in his diaper and training pants, Josh decided to snap him on the buttocks. He was protected by a thick diaper, but it made such a startling noise that the poor kid ran screaming back to his mother.

•••

WE'D ONLY BEEN IN Rapid City a week when my mother decided to talk Mrs. Coffee into utilizing her spacious trailer for a Thanksgiving dinner. She invited the juggler and his wife, the whip act and his wife, and the parents of both Josh and the kid he snapped on the diaper. None of us really knew each other that well. But my mother saw the opportunity to make a social event, and she took it.

On the night of the dinner Mrs. Coffee's table was exquisitely set with chinaware, silver, and embroidered cloth napkins of a kind I'd never seen before. There was even a kids table set just as elaborately. My father shaved his crop of whiskers and donned his best tailor-made apparel, all of which, combined with a parsimony of words, set him so far apart from the other trailer dwellers as to make him unapproachable. The only one missing was Tom Gary.

After we sat down, Bobbi and Mrs. Coffee transferred bowls and plates of food from the kitchen—including my mother's special stuffing, which was made from croutons, fig bars, and a touch of clam juice. Jean explained her husband's absence by saying, "He's out trying to find some horsemeat for the dog."

"Why horsemeat?" asked the father of the diaper kid who hugged his mother's leg and kept a suspicious eye on Josh.

"Oh, he has his reasons," she said.

"This is so unusual for us," said Josh's mother. "We've never met real circus people before."

"We're not with the circus," said Bobbi, coming up to her from behind with a platter of turkey. "We're in a higher class than that. Larry can juggle any three items the audience names, like a chair, a hanky, and a hat. He once performed for Eleanor Roosevelt."

From the kid's table I watched my father try to make small talk that came off as artificial as his skit with Clarabell. He was either overly theatrical, or at a total loss for words.

"Tell us about Eleanor Roosevelt," said Mrs. Coffee.

There was pounding on the door. It was Tom Gary. He stepped up into the trailer and his weight tilted it to one side. Everyone at the table had to move their chairs and plates to make room for his bulk.

"Find any horsemeat?" the diaper kid's father asked.

"A lotta live ones, but nothing dead. I did get some jackrabbit."

"How do you get that?"

"With this." He reached down the front of his pants and pulled out a pistol he thudded on the table. "My dog likes a wilder kind of meat. Otherwise he gets lazy and won't talk."

"Would you care for some tea?" asked Mrs. Coffee from the kitchen area.

"Just bring me a cup. I brought my own tea." He pulled a pint bottle of liquor from his back pocket and offered a snort to everyone, including the kid's table, but all declined. He turned to Mrs. Coffee back in the kitchen area.

"How about you, Mrs. Coffee? Coupla belts a this and you'll be dancing the Charleston. Whatta ya say?"

"I was raised to believe," she said, "that alcohol takes away a person's dignity." She approached the table with a platter of turkey. "Mr. Gary, if you could please remove your firearm, I will set this down and you may serve yourself."

He piled slice after slice onto his plate.

"Did we give you a knife?" she asked.

"Don't need one," he said, pronging a slab of white meat and gnawing it off his fork. He washed it down with what he poured in his teacup.

"Remember that knife thrower from Argentina?" he said with a mouthful of food. "The one who was half blind?"

The question was directed at the juggler and my father, so the trailer park people listened quietly and kept eating.

TOM GARY & CO.
You Will Get Comedy ala Mode

"One night he throws a knife and hits his assistant. Of course, the knives are dull and the backdrop is soft as a pound cake. The knife falls to the floor, but she gets a big bruise on the inside of her arm. During my act I can hear them yelling at each other in Spanish back in the dressing room. She beats him with a mop until it breaks then stabs him in the back with the sharp stub. It goes in pretty deep and he needs a doctor but it's a small town and they roll up the streets at night."

"What happened?" the diaper kid's mother asked.

"Nothing. His wife went around for a month with a big bruise on her arm, and he went around with a hole in his back."

Mrs. Coffee turned to my father. "Do you ever take spirits?"

"No, I do not. I was raised in a Baptist community in southern Indiana and everyone around me believed that liquor can cause great harm in a person's life." He seemed to be saying it more to himself than others at the table.

While Gary loaded his plate with more turkey, Mrs. Coffee turned to the juggler. "You mentioned Eleanor Roosevelt."

Before he had a chance to answer, Gary interrupted with his mouth still full of food. "I'm doing this show in Bismarck and some old bag starts heckling me. Hold on." He poured himself some more liquor and gulped it down. Then he belched with his mouth closed so his cheeks blew up like balloons, then released it with a powerful expulsion as everyone looked on with disgust.

"What are you looking at? I knew a guy who held back his belches because he was worried about being polite. You know what happened to him? He got stomach cancer and died."

"Tom, please, we're eating," said his wife.

"So I crack the bullwhip into a centerpiece of flowers at her table. Sounds like a goddamn cherry bomb going off in her face."

"Please!" said Mrs. Coffee. "Children are present."

"Leaves and petals fly everywhere. It shut her up, that's for *god*damn sure."

If the entertainers would have had their turkey and stuffing at a truck stop, everything would have been fine, but dinner in Mrs. Coffee's trailer seemed to unsettle everyone. I could feel it in the air. There were uneasy halts and prolonged silences. The diaper kid broke one of Mrs. Coffee's saltshakers and Josh started whining he wanted to leave. By the time Tom Gary emptied his bottle he was full of more bluster and burps than anyone could tolerate.

In the days that followed, someone complained to the trailer park manager that Tom Gary was using bad language in front of children. The diaper kid's mother took a great dislike to Mrs. Gary and said something hurtful to her at the clothes wringer. Gossip went around that the juggler made a pass at Josh's mother. No one wanted to see my mother's home movies anymore, and Mrs. Coffee grew cold.

One good thing came of it. The diaper kid warmed up to Josh again and his mother allowed them to play together as long as he did not leave the area around his trailer. When Josh and I went to the abandoned machine shop again we made the mistake of letting the diaper kid tag along. We jumped up and down on the rusted metal sheets over the pit and when the diaper kid did the same thing, he fell in. The greasy water in the pit was not as deep as we thought, so he did not sink over his head. We fished him out and he ran home howling, covered with oily muck. There was such an argument among the mothers that the trailer park manager had to step in. After that I wasn't allowed to play with Josh, and he wasn't allowed to play with me. The only time I saw him was through the trailer window in the morning walking with his mother to the washroom carrying the bucket.

"See what I mean about getting too close to people?" my whiskered father told my mother. "Sooner or later there's going to be trouble."

It was a relief to everyone when the Harvester Show tour started up as scheduled and we left Rapid City behind us.

As LONG AS I WAS not backstage or in the dressing room, there were few rules I had to follow. I could wander as far away as I pleased as long as I found my way back to the trailer by supper, which could be tricky if they moved it while I was gone. "Don't put your hand where you can't see your fingers," my father warned me. "If a dog comes at you, stand still, never run. And don't touch used chewing gum because there might be syphilis on it."

If we parked for a few days at a gas station and I complained about having no friends, he'd tell me, "Knock on some doors and say, 'Do you have any kids I can play with?'"

I was always cautious of houses because they seemed like such strange places. The few times I ventured into the bizarre immobility known as someone else's *house*, I was intimidated by stairs that went down into some kind of darkness below or an inscrutable elevation above. There was an overabundance of space and doors leading to more space. House dwellers could be just as cautious of me. If a kid's parents found out I lived in a trailer, there was concern. I knew what they meant when they said after a short while putting up with me, "Don't you think it's time for you to go home?"

My father knocked on the doors of theatrical agents all the time, most of whom were not interested, but if he didn't keep doing it there would be nothing to eat every night when I returned to the trailer. If I were to make something of myself someday, I might as well start early and get used to knocking on those doors. There weren't always a lot of doors to knock on, and people who answered would either say no, there are no kids here to play with, or they'd lavish pity on me. Either way, there was no one to play with. One time a man tried to lure me into his house, saying *he* would play with me, but there was something a little too friendly about him, so I declined his offer.

When I told my father, he said, "Did you go in?"

"No."

"That's good. You did the right thing. Adult strangers don't invite little boys into their house to play. They're crazy people who get that way because of the War. All you can do is stay away from them. Remember, if anyone chases you, run in a zigzag like a rabbit. They'll run out of energy before they get close. And if they do get close, crouch down suddenly and they'll trip right over you. Then get up and keep running in zigzags."

No adult ever ran after me, but other kids sometimes did, and his zigzag technique worked beautifully.

Whenever he "spotted" the trailer—that is, parked it in a central place—it was either for purposes of layover or to drive out to engagements alone in an ever-increasing radius until he had to move it again. When I asked him when he was coming back, the answer was never definite. I'd watch his car drive off and then disappear down the highway. I regarded this as another example he set for me. If he could suddenly head for some place like Sioux City, why couldn't I? One day at Cole's Trailer Park in Des Moines, I got on my tricycle and pedaled down the highway in the same direction. I remember the thrill of taking off and the ease of peddling on solid pavement instead of the usual trailer park dirt and gravel. Honking cars and trucks backed up behind me. I don't remember who it was that snatched me, trike and all, off the highway, or what the consequences were after that, but I remember having no motivation to do it again.

On a tricycle, at least.

Then there was school. With plenty of hours in the back seat of the car with nothing else to do, I taught myself to read. I took correspondence courses and learned to write forward or backward with either hand. If we were in a town longer than a few days, my father tried to enroll me in a local school, explaining he was a magician on tour, but the show biz smile and spiffy duds didn't get either of us very far. There were forms to fill out, records to transfer, and all the rest. He decided to change tactics.

"This is where you're going to have to be a big boy. Follow the other kids and go where they go. Walk into the office and stand up straight with your shoulders back and your head up and tell them your name. Say, 'I want to go to school here.' Don't mumble. Hold out your hand and always shake with a strong grip. Let me feel that handshake. That's good, but a little stronger. There you go. You can't be afraid of new situations. If you think that way, you'll never make anything of yourself."

After the War there were an estimated 12,000 trailer parks in the US, most of them full of young families with kids, so it was not unusual for schools to encounter children with shifty backgrounds. Showing up in a white shirt and tie and shaking hands and expressing a desire to go to school worked quite well in small communities that had their own practical means of accommodation. They went ahead and put me in a classroom. Before they could decide what to do after that I'd be gone.

After attending so many schools in this manner I learned I could invent a lie in one place and transport it to another, reworking and perfecting it each time. Kids didn't believe me when I said my father was a magician. "How do we know you're not lying?" They were right. It was a hard thing to prove. If I said he sold insurance, they believed that without question and didn't try to taunt the truth out of me.

I had other fibs, too. On the playground I'd show some kid a photo of Hopalong Cassidy I picked up when he and my father appeared together. It was not signed, so I signed it myself. "Don't tell anyone." I knew kids could not keep a secret so the next day, as I expected, all the other kids wanted to see it and I got the acceptance I was looking for. Eventually they would have figured out the ruse by comparing the fake signature to one on a Hopalong Cassidy lunch box, but I'd be gone by then, working the same routine at another school. I became my own little Master of Deception.

•••

HOUSES ARE MEANT TO be seen, but not trailers. They're backstage stuff. No one wanted to be reminded of them, so they were kept as far out of sight as possible along with factories and dumps. Or, better yet, not allowed at all. In one such town without a trailer park we stayed behind a gas station until we were no longer welcome, then moved to where a farmer rented us a space behind his barn next to a pasture with a few cows and a pony.

"I'd like to keep it down to a week or so," said the farmer. "And you gotta be quiet because too much commotion bothers the cows. I rented to a guy a while back who had a dog that howled funny and got all the other dogs a mile around howling too. He liked to crack whips outside his trailer. Spooked the cattle something awful. Had a fowl mouth on him, too. I had to tell him to move on."

My father assured him we'd be quiet, then hooked up to the electricity with the extra-long extension cord we always kept in the outside compartment at the rear of the trailer. We kept the rabbit and birds in the car so the farm dogs wouldn't eat them. The next day he said, "Okay, let's find you a school." Since there were no trailer park kids to follow, he drove me into town and found the elementary school. "Take a good look at the landmarks and remember where they are when you go there yourself tomorrow. When you get to the highway, turn past the bar and look for the fence and the pony in the pasture."

The next morning, I walked down the highway into town with my lunch in a bag, making note of the landmarks my father pointed out. In the office I threw my shoulders back, held my head high, thrust out my hand, and introduced myself. As usual, they found me a desk in a classroom, then tried to figure out who the devil I was and what to do with me.

My place in the lesson plan varied from town to town. I might be way ahead in Dodge City, but way behind in Abilene. I could be the smartest kid in the class in Cimarron and the dumbest in Wellington. I was either catching up or breezing by. The deciding factor in whether I liked a new school was the age of my teacher. The younger ones were my favorites since they tended to be idealistic and enjoyed teaching. The older ones could be joyless and strict, having long since given up, like kiddie entertainers, any illusions about the innocent nature of children.

I was assigned to a teacher I'll call Mrs. Proctor who had wild gray hair and a burning gaze. When she asked me why I was late I tried to explain, but she cut me off.

"Did you use the lavatory yet?"

"No."

"Do you have to use the lavatory now?"

"No."

Each school had its own fixation on a single behavior. In Texas it was biting. "No biting!" the teachers kept yelling at everyone during recess, but when I came home, I had teeth marks on my arms and legs. At another school it was "no throwing!" The playground happened to be full of rocks kids could not resist picking up, and every so often someone broke a window or was hit on the head. Here it was "the lavatory." All day I heard teachers tell the kids, "Use the lavatory!"

I sat next to a wiggly boy, whom I'll call Roger, and a hefty girl wearing pants under her dress, whom I remember as "Big Sheila." Mrs. Proctor continued with what she'd been saying before my tardy arrival. "Now listen, people. Nap time means putting your heads down and keeping your eyes closed. You don't peek at your neighbor. Since you're all looking at the new pupil who just walked in, let's everyone say hello."

They all said hello in unison.

"Did you just move here?" she asked.

"Yes."

"Where did you live before?"

"I don't know." A few kids laughed. "Before" could mean any one of a hundred places on that year's Harvester Show tour.

"All right, people, we have to understand how confusing it must be to move to a new town. What does your daddy do?"

"He sells insurance."

"People, button those lips. Roger, button the lip."

Roger made a buttoning gesture with his fingers.

"All right, get out your music books."

Mrs. Proctor sat down at her piano and told us to turn to a page. She played and everyone sang. Everyone except for me. Music was the only subject I truly did not like. In retrospect I can understand the educational value of learning songs and singing in a group, but as I sat in Mrs. Proctor's classroom, I could not see the point. I was around musicians all the time. My father had a folder of stage music and rehearsing the orchestra was part of every show. Billy Papon played various sized harmonicas, including the tiny one he swallowed. Dick Weston, the ventriloquist, could drink a glass of milk while the dummy sang. Professor Merrill's trombone fell apart as he played it. That all that made sense, but singing together in a classroom did not.

During recess I joined Roger, Big Sheila, and a few older boys in a game where they circled around each other in a wide arc and then, on no particular signal, ran headlong into each other in a powerful body slam. Clearly not a game for everyone. Sheila was the most enthusiastic player, and I became her favorite target. She took special delight in running as fast as she could and knocking me to the ground, which I very much enjoyed.

When school was out, kids got on buses or walked home. I went along with Roger and some others who stopped at a tree in front of a house and made great sport of throwing leftover sandwiches up as high as they could, watching them fly apart in midair, lunchmeat sailing one way, bread slices the other. Black banana peels hung in the branches. When a man's frowning face appeared in the window, we ran away laughing, leaving food scraps all over the corner of his yard. I was having so much fun I almost forgot I had a home to return to. Not only that, but I wasn't quite sure where that home was, even though my father pointed out landmarks I was supposed to remember. There were so many towns and so many landmarks they all ran together. I eventually found my way to the bar and then the pasture where the pony grazed along the fence. In the distance I saw the trailer tongue with two propane tanks sticking out from behind the barn. As I walked toward it, the pony followed me along the fence, and when I stopped to stroke its twitchy muzzle it caught my necktie in its teeth and started to chew it.

•••

"TODAY WE'RE GOING TO learn about our neighbors," said Mrs. Proctor. "You will draw a picture of the person who lives next door to you. Then you will write something about that person."

Students applied their crayons to sheets of art paper, occasionally looking over to see what the others were doing. When finished, we took turns holding up our drawings and explaining what we did. Part of the lesson was to fill in verbally what we didn't express in the drawing. "He is fun" meant the neighbor played catch and was a Little League coach. "She makes cukies," written under a head covered with squiggly hair, referred to Gramma, who made oatmeal cookies. Roger drew a crude automobile and only got as far as "car..." as he explained that his neighbor had an old Ford with a loud muffler that released a lot of smoke. On Sheila's page was a smiling face connected by a line to an oval body with four legs and a tail. Next to it she wrote, "The dog liks me," and explained how her dog jumped up to lick her face when she came home from school.

As long as the pupils drew something and put down at least a couple or three words, Mrs. Proctor considered the assignment complete. For that they got a red star on the page, which they could take home and show their parents and maybe the neighbor they wrote about. Some students only managed to come up with a drawing but couldn't put down so much as a single word. They didn't get a red star. Then she called on me.

"Neighbor" was a concept I didn't fully understand. I could have drawn the farmer but didn't know his name or anything about him. Forgetting my father was supposed to be an insurance salesman, I drew a fat man holding a bullwhip wrapped around someone's face. Under the drawing I wrote, "I take yor hed off."

I often assumed, incorrectly, that other children were familiar with the same things I was, like sway poles and simul-talkers. And they assumed I knew about such things as basements and next-door neighbors. Trying to describe Tom Gary as the man next door quickly became a muddle. "Comedy a la Mode" was hard enough to explain even by a theatrical agent. "He does funny stuff with a bullwhip," was about all they could say, even though what he did, like wrapping it around someone's face, was not always funny. All I did was convince Mrs. Proctor that I was a confused child who didn't know where he came from and had disturbing thoughts of someone taking off someone's head. All the students, even the ones who couldn't think of anything to write, brought their drawings home, but not me. Mrs. Proctor kept mine, maybe for the principal, maybe for the school nurse. What I got instead was a note to my parents, and to make sure it got to them she attached it to the front of my shirt with a safety pin.

72

On my way home Roger let me smash his left-over orange against a tree with a thrilling splat. The man whose yard we littered every day ran out the door and yelled at us as we ran down the street laughing. Roger went into his house and I continued back to the trailer, following the landmarks I now knew. But they did not matter anymore because this would be my last day attending school in that town. I would never see Roger again, or Sheila or Mrs. Proctor or the pony grazing next to me along the fence where it tried to extend its head through to the other side. It nuzzled my arm and nibbled at my shirt, then pulled off the note and ate it.

SECOND ATTRACTION

APPEARANCES

BURLESQUE TODAY IS FEATURED in the form of what Eliot called (referring to something else) "artificially sustained antiquarianism." You can take classes in burlesque dancing along with belly dance or yoga. It's all for fun and empowerment. There's a collector's market for marquee photos, coffee-table books, and costumes. When my father pulled our trailer into the Twin Cities, burlesque clubs were a thriving marketplace of solid demand that created a livelihood for many people. Yet there was nothing empowering about working them. They were rowdy and full of hecklers. Drunks were known to rush the stage. A dancer might have to pry filthy hands off her body while the audience cheered and laughed until the bouncers came to her rescue. The pay was low, but the work was plentiful. It would form the beginning of that strange state of affairs I would come to know as permanence.

Most of the performers we knew, even yodelers and balloon artists, worked in burlesque clubs at least occasionally. They gave such venues a chance to show good faith to licensing authorities by appearing to be more than dens of primal urge. On a more practical level they provided an interval between dance sets so the strippers could change costumes. Although acts went out of their way to advertise themselves as "clean," they made minor concessions in strip clubs. A juggler might joke about his "balls," or the Prince of Pantomime might throw in a "damn" or "hell" just to try and fit it in. Or, if they were incapable of even that, they simply worked clean, like my parents, and took their chances. My father beamed his million-dollar smile and pulled cards out of the air to chants of "bring on the girls!" and when my mother came out in her usual high heels and fishnet stockings for the trunk escape, there were whistles and catcalls. To the management, heckling was the sound of money. If customers didn't pay attention to the show, they bought drinks. All that mattered was staying out there for twenty minutes no matter what. Cutting it short meant the dancers wouldn't have enough time to change, and no one wanted to find out what happens when you rush a half-dressed stripper.

The ventriloquist, Grover Ruwe, went further than most in adapting to burlesque clubs and actually created a demand for himself. He was known to everyone by his last name only, pronounced "Rooey." If he got heckled, the dummy heckled back, raw and risqué. Hence, Ruwe and Louie were billed as "Tops in Backtalk," and they could demolish a room. The dummy threw insults and broke all taboos. Strip club patrons actually forgot about the dancers as they doubled over helpless, pounding the tables in uncontrollable laughter.

Even though he was often in town, he lived in a trailer of his own in Kansas City with an ex-stripper named Barbara Kelly and their toddler son. He was a regular visitor at our trailer in Minneapolis. If I brought over some of the trailer park kids, he did the trick where it looked like he was pulling off the tip of his thumb. Except in Ruwe's case he didn't have a thumb. He lost it (plus an index finger) in a woodworking accident. When he showed them the stub, it was so shocking the kids ran away and left him alone.

At burlesque clubs my parents restricted me to the dressing room because the sight of a young boy among the clientele would be unseemly and have a dampening effect on the audience, not to mention the strippers. But I was no problem in the dressing room, where the Lovely Sylvia, the Exciting Cynthia, Exotic Star Dolly Malone, René ("dancing the way you like it"), Thrilling May Louise, Sizzling Conchita, and the Daring Lavodis walked around more naked than before their howling fans. I was invisible, as trained, and everyone else had more important things to worry about. Long before I started school my mother brought me into the women's showers, so I had seen it all before. Adult women, as far as I was concerned, strippers or otherwise, all had bodies more or less like my mother. If I did happen to glance thrusting hips or breasts swinging with tassels, they were merely standard stunts, like balancing a chair on the chin, or standing on one hand. Once in a while, out of stage fright, one might turn me into a living worry bead and stroke my hair while waiting to go out and give a bunch of liquored up buckaroos "a little something they can't get at home."

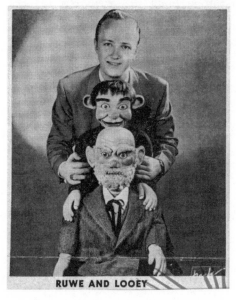

RUWE AND LOOEY

•••

WE STAYED AT SEVERAL trailer parks in the Twin Cities, with trailers lined up side-by-side under the bare sky, until a spot opened at the more scenic Oak Grove Trailer Park in the suburb of New Brighton. Most trailers did not have telephones, so if someone received a call, it first came into the office, then the manager made an announcement over a loudspeaker to the whole park. Since my father received calls from scores of theatrical agencies, his name was announced more often than anyone else's. He'd burst from our trailer or the washroom, sometimes with shaving cream over his face, running on bowed legs to get that all-important call.

Oak Grove had its usual share of fearsome recluses who were the way they were *because of the War*, and kids knew better than to go near their trailers. In fact, the trailer park itself existed because of the War. Most of its inhabitants worked at a place known as "the Arsenal," a World War II weapons plant that afterward became a disassembly site for the enormous stockpile of ordinance left over. When the Russians set off their first atomic bomb, the Arsenal reverted back to assembling weapons again. It became a human anthill where thousands labored day and night, and what went on within its huge complex of 250 buildings was so secret that in the event of an accident, ambulance medics couldn't go in but had to wait for the victim or victims to be carried out whole or in parts. With the expansion of the Arsenal came the expansion of the trailer park until it filled to capacity and there was a long waiting list. We were lucky to get in before the Russians found the secret to the Bomb.

New Brighton Elementary was the first school where I was legitimately enrolled, and every day I joined an army of children who walked a half mile to get there. War was an issue at school, too. In class they showed us films of mushroom clouds and fake houses with mannequins blown over by walls of fire. We practiced crouching under our desks in the event such a thing should happen to us. Fear was everywhere. According to Senator McCarthy, the Communists were already here. In the trailer, while rehearsing card maneuvers, my father watched red-scare programs on our small Sentinel TV, like *Passport to Danger, Foreign Intrigue,* and *I Led Three Lives.*

At my new school I had to learn yet one more set of rules. I followed them but also figured out how they might be dodged, something that had always served me well and would continue to do so in the years to come. I still wandered off the school grounds if I could get away with it and invited myself into the boiler room to say hi to the janitor, but I could no longer fabricate stories on the playground in the expectation of leaving town in a day or two. My teacher, Miss Birdsill, recently started teaching and was patient with me even though she didn't know what to make of what I said or did, like the time I brought an unusually powerful industrial magnet to class for show-and-tell. Billy Papon had picked it up at a banquet for a manufacturing company and gave it to me. It attracted (like himself) at a distance. Miss Birdsill wanted me to tell about the person who gave me the magnet. I tried to explain the Prince of Pantomime.

"He tips the mic stand over to bring it close to the record player, then moves his lips to the words of the 'Barber of Seville' while his hair falls over the front of his face. He's got boxes of dinosaur eggs in the trunk of his car and swallows this little harmonica when he…"

"Okay," said Miss Birdsill. "Let's see the magnet."

I held up the thick slab and brought it to a metal cabinet door. I felt its tug begin a few inches away and then, with a loud thump, it clamped itself so tightly I couldn't pull it off. Neither could Miss Birdsill. She tried to make this an educational experience by asking the class what they had learned from my demonstration. "Don't put magnets on doors," someone said. After that no one paid attention to anyone else during show-and-tell because they kept staring at the magnet stuck to the door. In order to conduct the class without distraction, Miss Birdsill had to have the janitor come in and remove it with a crowbar.

It stuck to that too.

•••

I ATTENDED SCHOOL BY day and accompanied my parents to engagements by night. I watched my father rehearse his background music with the orchestra ("give me cymbal crash and a chord"), line up the bill as emcee, deliver a canned intro for each act, then do what he was hired to do. I learned the routines of Earl Dunn ("Man with a Thousand Voices"), Harris Nelson ("the Entertaining Maestro"), Roy Pratt and Helene ("Mind Readers Extraordinaire"), and, of course, "Tops in Backtalk" and "the Prince of Pantomime." I became equally familiar with the service entrances and back halls and stairways of downtown hotels where banquets were held, like the Curtis, the Leamington, the Radisson, and the Dyckman, as if they were the rooms of one big estate. I saw singers, dancers, a roller skating couple who spun in circles on a small platform (he went to prison for murdering his former partner), Jose Colé, who could stand on one finger (wearing a trick glove), knock-about acts, drunk acts, trained dogs, chimps, cockatoos, and a man who did six minutes taking off an absurd number of layers of clothes that he gathered up and stuffed back in his baggy pants. I saw them in glorious triumph and spectacular defeat. I saw them perform so sick they should have been in bed, if not the hospital, and so exhausted they could barely make it back to their car, only to drive all night to another engagement.

Extended stay in any trailer park increased the chances of eventually moving into a coveted hook-up spot close to the washroom. That would mean less distance to carry laundry and walk with wet hair in the cold after using the showers. There weren't many transients at Oak Grove because work at the Arsenal was steady and permanent, but a spot next to the washroom did open and we took it. Since the office, as usual, was next to the washroom, my father did not have to run as far on his bad legs to answer phone calls. The manager sent over his four-year-old daughter to knock on our door and announce in her little voice, "telephone!" thus removing the constant annoyance of his name broadcast to the entire park.

•••

MY PARENTS WERE THE most prosperous-looking people in Oak Grove, although probably the lowest paid despite working the longest hours. One might wonder why, for appearing so affluent and driving a new car (always covered with highway dirt), they lived in an old Travelo with no bathroom. Since we had come into a state of tentative permanence, my mother obtained charge plates for Dayton's, Donaldson's, and Young-Quinlin's in downtown Minneapolis, where she brought me along to keep her company while shopping. I pushed my way into the racks of hanging dresses with dangling tags while she lost herself in glorious indecision over what to buy and bring back to our already packed trailer.

Accompanying my father to buy clothes was a different experience. At Mr. Kuppleman's tailor shop, garments were in their indeterminate form as bolts of material on high shelves reachable only by a stepladder. With my father there was no indecision. He knew exactly what he wanted before he walked in for a complicated fitting procedure.

Mr. Kuppleman had a ghostly appearance and I must have been one of those kids that adults try to ignore as they stare and keep staring. He was an older man with a large, shiny head. His movements were slow and precise, and he spoke with a thick accent as he directed my father to stand on a platform like a small stage, complete with spotlights shining down at different angles.

He too was in the business of concealment and knew about physical deformities and how to hide them. My father may have possessed the face of a matinee idol and the torso of a gymnast, but from the waist down he had what is known medically as genu varum, or bowed legs. Mr. Kuppleman constructed an ingenious drape for each pant leg with a knife-sharp crease of perfect vertical plumb to hide the condition. He created secret pockets and undetectable places behind the lapels for birds in their snap-open pouches. It took more than the usual number of visits. In the process of measuring and inserting rows of pins, his shirt cuff rode up just enough to reveal a series of tattooed numbers on his forearm like the ones I'd see in the ears of rabbits my father bought from commercial breeders.

After we left the shop, I asked my father, "Why does Mr. Kuppleman have those numbers tattooed on his arm?"

"You must never say a word about that. Not to Mr. Kuppleman or anyone else."

"Because of the War?"

"Because of the War."

That was the explanation for everything that could not be explained. Why Peg Leg Bates tap danced on one leg. Why a tailor had numbers tattooed on his arm. Why crazy men flew out of their trailers yelling at kids.

We returned to the shop, and Mr. Kuppleman continued sculpting his sartorial art upon my father. He pinched a cluster of pins to one side of his mouth and spoke out the other. "Is the boy going to follow in father's footsteps?" His accent made the words roll around like shells churned by a wave.

"No, he's going to make something of himself."

I never understood my father's answer to that commonly asked question. Why should he debase himself like that? After all, he was on TV before we even owned one, and his picture was often in the paper. He performed on the same stage as Frank Sinatra and appeared with Clarabell the Clown. Everyone in the trailer park knew his name from hearing it so many times over the loudspeaker. Had he not made something of himself?

Mr. Kuppleman addressed me directly without looking. "What are you most interested in, Mr. Jack Junior?... Bend the other leg slightly, thank you... Science, did you say? That's good. My nephew comes in here afternoons and helps me with alterations. He doesn't have any interests. All he does is what he's told. That's not so good when you only do what you're told. He wants to run my business when I retire, but he can't think ahead. Last month he's taking up a cuff and suddenly gets the hiccups and swallows a pin. Anyone with the hiccups should be careful of pins in the mouth. Not him. He's in the hospital two days while they follow the pin through his system. Can you imagine what that was like? Fortunately, they didn't have to operate. To make a proper suit you need to focus ahead and see the finished result. For you, science. Very good. Focus on science."

People were fond of giving me advice, and since I met lots of people, I got lots of advice. Gene Autry told me to "ride high in the saddle," whatever that was supposed to mean. Sophie Tucker said that when I grew up, I should watch out for "fast women." I wasn't sure about that one either. Was it the Big Sheilas of the world coming at me "fast" and knocking me to the ground? But not all adults had advice. Hank Williams didn't have any, nor did Julius La Rosa, Hopalong Cassidy, or Clarabell. The best advice I ever got was from my father telling me to shake hands with a firm grip and don't touch gum under restaurant tables.

When Mr. Kuppleman was finally through with his creation upon the pedestal, my father was ready to go forth as a walking mass of concealment. From a distance, under lights, his carefully constructed suit of tails draped his slender physique perfectly, while hiding birds, a collapsible cage, an appearing cane on a hair-trigger ready to spring into existence, and an egg coated in floor wax so it would slide easily out of its specially designed pocket. When fully rigged, ready to appear before an audience, he was one of Mr. Kuppleman's greatest creations. But to jump into his arms at that point would have been a catastrophe.

•••

I'D SEEN ALL KINDS of wardrobe, from sequined pubic patches to a full suit of tails, but nothing like what I saw one day on someone who descended from the heavens and entered our trailer. He wore an immaculate military officer's uniform covered with shiny, eye-fixating medals—some of them hinged in two parts. One whole side of his chest was aligned with rows of bars in vertical bands of color, like the best specimens of Lake Superior agate. His shoes were especially striking and polished even beyond Mr. Rhythm's tap shoes, obsidian black with pinpoints of light beaming from the toes. They seemed above stepping on earthly ground. There was no advance mention of his visit. My father said he was going to the train station to pick him up, and an hour later there he was, the myth, the words in a prayer, sitting across from me—an unbelievable sight at the drop table in our little trailer.

A few nights earlier there was great excitement over what was on the evening news. "There he is!" my father said. "It's called the F-100, the first fighter jet to break the sound barrier. It's made from some new kind of metal." It happened so quickly I barely saw the slant-winged projectile shoot across our small black and white TV screen. His name wasn't mentioned, but Big Brother Jerry was supposed to have been the pilot of that plane.

He had apparently been transferred from Kadena Air Force Base in Okinawa and was now stationed at Seymour Johnson Air Force Base in North Carolina, where he was a test pilot. He must have landed one of the jets at Ellsworth Air Force Base in Rapid City where, if the timing were different, he could have met us when we were there a few months earlier. He decided to take the train to Minneapolis even though by jet it was just down the street.

Taller, with rounded facial features and a husky body, he didn't resemble my father except for an easy manner and a shy version of the smile I only saw on stage. It never occurred to me what it must have been like for him to meet the woman who took away his father, whom he never saw on stage doing what was considered by many in Spencer County the work of the Devil. He never traveled outside Spencer County, Indiana, until he joined the Air Force, and after that he saw the world mostly from the air.

"The danger," he said, "is not so much flying the F-100 as in trying to land. It's built for speed. The slower you go, and the closer you get to the ground, the more likely you are to crash. The safest place to be is high and fast as possible. Any pilot will tell you that for all the work and all the danger there's no greater thrill than sitting in that cockpit and flying into the blue faster than sound. The sense of freedom is beyond belief."

I told him that my favorite carnival ride was the Spitfire, mechanical planes that could be maneuvered to roll. I knew just how to do it so that they'd roll over continuously. On each ride there was always one plane that went over more easily than the others and all the carnie kids knew which plane that was.

"I've never been to a carnival," said Jerry.

This was a profound statement. All those summers I played with carnie kids, went on rides, ran through funhouses, and saw all the sideshows for free—that was something he'd never known. And yet we had the same father. For me our father was always going away and returning from somewhere unknown. In Jerry's case he went away to somewhere unknown and never came back.

"The feel of that ride you just mentioned sounds close to what it's like to fly a real plane. Can you imagine going so fast it takes five miles just to turn around?"

I knew it was not easy to turn around with a trailer either, and sometimes on a small county road it took almost that distance before it was possible. That's why the wrong shortcut on dirt roads could end up taking longer.

"A jet can turn around on a dime, but the gravitational force on the pilot would knock him out. Defeats the whole purpose, right? There's an old saying, the plane can take more stress than the pilot."

"And a car," my mother joined in, "can take more stress than the driver."

"Man and machine. They'll never be equals. How fast do you travel with the trailer?"

"About forty miles per hour," my father said. "On an open road we can get up to sixty, but beyond that the trailer starts to fishtail."

"Speed and stability. The whole history of travel. Even if a horse gallops, it runs a risk of stumbling." He turned to me. "You too. I bet you've fallen down more often running than walking. That's why they say walk, don't run. Are you good at math?"

My gaps in learning addition and subtraction corresponded to my gaps in attending school, and I still have to do certain calculations on my fingers. Jerry took out a fountain pen and found a scrap of paper.

"If you go forty miles per hour pulling your trailer, you will go about two-thirds of a mile in one minute. See? Divide forty by sixty. If you were in a jet, in one minute you'd go this far." He showed me the envelope with the answer circled. "Think you could run that fast?"

"Ten miles? In one minute? How long would it take to fly to the moon?"

"In a jet, let's see…rounding it off it would be…around three hundred hours and that would come to…roughly two weeks. Want to go some day?"

As the afternoon progressed, Jerry shared with me an enthusiasm for small amusements. He put one hand on top of the other and waved his thumbs like the wings of a bird. He held a pencil loosely between his thumb and first finger then shook it up and down so it looked like it was made of rubber. He ran a finger up a certain vein on his arm, making it disappear, then lifted it so the blood flow popped it back up again. When I was older and my veins became prominent enough, I discovered the same vein on my own arm and found that I too could make it go flat and pop up again. I have never impressed anyone with it, but then I've never done it as an incarnated ghost.

That night, at one of the hotels downtown where I knew every stairwell and passageway, Jerry saw my father perform for the first time. It was a private matter that did not involve my mother or myself. I would never know what Jerry thought about my—*his*—father pulling cards out of the air and doing tricks he didn't know the secrets to. It was never discussed in my presence. When they returned to the trailer Jerry slept in my room and I slept with my parents in the foldout bed. With dressing room stealth, I spied him removing his medal-laden coat and hanging it on a hanger on the knob of my closet door. Keeping the knot intact, he carefully unloosened his tie just enough to pull it over his head. He unbuttoned only the top few buttons of his starched and ironed shirt then carefully slipped it off like a shell. The lights went out and there we were, as close as we'd ever get to the whole family together.

I still didn't know where Jerry came from except TV, the sky, or both. I never had to deal with a little brother or sister coming from "mommy's tummy." I knew where cards and birds and rabbits came from, but not babies. I just assumed you went to the hospital, like going to a rabbit breeder, and picked one up.

Before my father took him back to the train station Jerry walked with me around the swampy area outside the park, stepping carefully over the ground with his shined shoes, not letting the slightest smudge get upon them. With his pocketknife he showed me how to cut a

Y-shaped branch from a tree and then strips of rubber from an old inner tube we found in the trash. All the while he preserved the spotless perfection of his uniform. Like magic he created a slingshot that could propel a rock so high into the air it disappeared. And then he was gone.

After that I looked at anything airborne in a different way. Every contrail, every airplane banner, every sonic boom and skywritten word. When I pumped myself high as possible on a playground swing, I felt I was approaching Jerry out there, up there, in or above the clouds, where phantom half-brothers come from.

•••

"I NEED A DECENT place to hang my clothes," my mother said. "I need a *decent* kitchen. And I can't tell you how sick I am of that damned bucket. I want a *decent* bathroom!"

She might have tolerated these privations in pursuit of her own career in the theater, but it was different being the unnamed "lovely assistant." Since novelty entertainment was supposed to be about money, at least she wanted something to show for her hardship. The average cost of a house in the early 1950s was around $17,000. There was no way my father could come up with a fraction of that for his lovely assistant to live decently, since card-pulling and rabbit-dangling was not where the money was. If he enjoyed status at a banker's convention with his "suave good humor" and "clever tricks," when it came to a loan, he was a leper. A God-knows-what. When not in Cimarron or Memphis or Sioux City, he sat in our trailer and carefully studied Hubbard Cobb's *Your Dream Home: How to Build It for Less than $3,500* (1950). The drop-leaf table was covered with papers and calculations, columns of numbers, product brochures, and pictures my mother cut from magazines. He studied Cobb's drab gray volume with its side indents like a dictionary, marking topics like "Getting Started," "Foundations," and "Framing." He wedged so many cutouts and notes between the pages that the book's binding began to fall apart. I didn't dare touch it, not so much for fear of dropping it and losing all the place markers, but because it represented the end of life as I knew it.

To build this imagined house, he exercised his own father's Baptist work ethic and booked ever more burlesque clubs. I went along on these engagements until a certain problem arose. Child Protection started sending spies into strip clubs to make sure no underage hoofers or acrobats worked as alternating acts. I'm sure that went for a magician's kid too. If they came into a dressing room and saw me folding dove bags while the Daring Lovadis snugged up a G-string, I might end up in a foster home and have to follow some really different rules. For the first time in my life I was exposed to that tribe of gum crackers known as "babysitters."

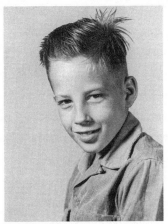

A girl named Audrey, daughter of the janitor who pried Billy Papon's magnet off the door, had put up a notice in the trailer park washroom advertising her services. I could tell the moment she entered that I would like her. In the trailer there was no requirement I be invisible, so hardly had my parents driven away when I was rolling around at her feet. She let me play with the ends of her nylons stretched over lacquered toenails and soon I was on the davenport, exploring the rest of her. She was taller and heavier than my mother and wore a sweater soft as rabbit fur over shoulders that were all flesh and no bone. I buried my face in her neck and breathed her in as if to inhale her completely. Where my mother was at best tolerant of this sort of thing, Audrey was open to it, and perhaps even encouraging. If I was going to be left behind, I made it worth my while. The next time my parents performed some place I wasn't allowed, they tried substituting her with another babysitter, a kindly grandmother with a bun and enormous low-hanging ears. I made such a fuss that they had to bring back Audrey, like the Daring Lovadis, by popular demand.

•••

ONE DAY MY FATHER did the unthinkable. He brought a Negro into the trailer park. Any non-Caucasian with the temerity to set foot in the land of Airstreams, Vindales, and Stuart Coaches would be regarded as disturbing the peace. As this alien creature stepped up into our wheeled house, people stood dumbfounded or peeked through the blinds of their front windows. His name was Teddy Qualls, the tap dancer known as "Mr. Rhythm." He needed a ride to Fargo, where he and my father were booked at the same Elks Club. But for Mr. Rhythm it was a much different situation.

He and his twin brother were born in New York City and raised as orphans in Father Flanagan's Boys Town in Nebraska. His twin went into a life of crime and ended up in prison under the White

Slave Traffic Act for running prostitutes across state lines. Teddy saved himself by going into show business.

His publicity brochure described him as "the protégé of Paul Robeson," the African American singer who made the hit recording of "Old Man River" from *Showboat* and starred as Othello at the Savoy Theater in London. It was only the drop of a famous name because Robeson and Qualls were in no way similar.

Before the audience knew who he was, the emcee introduced Qualls as "a real live Scandinavian folk dancer." Then, to everyone's shock and laughter, he jumped from behind the curtain, as out of place as a piece of coal in a bag of marshmallows. Facing a stunned audience, he forced out a loud guffaw, showed big white teeth and eyes bugged out as if to say, *Ha! Looga this, white folks!* With his checkered coat and trilby hat on a bobbing head, he played the Negro stereotype to the point of absolute hilarity. Like a good stripper will burlesque sex, Mr. Rhythm burlesqued race. I heard a theatrical agent one time try to sell him over the phone. "He's a colored boy who devastates—I mean *devastates*—an audience. Even if you don't like the coloreds, this jigaboo will knock 'em outta their damn chairs!"

It was no exaggeration. After his initial impression as a walking sight gag, he tipped the mic stand over so the microphone was on the floor to better pick up the sound of huge Stevens Stomper steel taps screwed into the heel and toe of his patent leather shoes. Then he lunged his way around the stage in a blitzkrieg of self-deprecating racial mockery. *You better laugh, or I'm gonna move right next door to you!* He had an abnormal number of sweat glands and almost from the beginning, generous plewds of perspiration flew in all directions. His biggest laugh (remember, this was the 1950s) was when he wiped his face with a handkerchief and said, *Looga all that good hot chocolate goin' to waste!* He did a solid twenty minutes and that was it. True to the agent's promise, he did knock 'em outta their damn chairs. When he left the stage, the show was over. No one could follow something like that. Talent and success don't always go together, but Qualls did have one chance at fame when he was selected as opening act for Bob Hope on one of his tours. The problem was, Mr. Rhythm was too good. He got bigger laughs than the famous comedian.

So they fired him.

There were two reasons why he was riding to Fargo with us. One, he was a notoriously bad driver and frequently got lost, drove the wrong way down one-way streets, or mistook a sidewalk for a road. Small-town cops gave him little sympathy as a black man, although his comedy skills occasionally got him off the hook. The other reason was because he sometimes got turned away on racial grounds from the very places that hired him. The agent would have to call the client and it could take a while to resolve the matter. His mentor, Paul Robeson, ran into the same problem, fame notwithstanding. I often heard the story of the time Robeson tried to check into the Curtis Hotel in Minneapolis, where he had a reservation. The desk clerk took one look at him and tried to say there were no rooms available. Robeson had a law degree from Columbia University and was an ex-professional football tackle, so he was not only articulate but physically imposing. He slammed his giant fist down on the desk and corrected the bigoted fool in no uncertain terms. He got his room with no further delay. Teddy was gentle and nonconfrontational. He was better off with us. To turn him away meant they'd have to turn us away too—white people— and how dreadful would that be?

While my mother, who always needed more time, was getting ready in the trailer, we picked him up at his house, which, of course, was in a black neighborhood. His shy wife stood in the doorway to see him off as everyone on the block stared at us, as out of place as a Negro in a trailer park, and watched their talented neighbor get in a car with white people who carried him off to the heart of darkness.

My father rearranged the back seat to make room for Teddy and me. Like Billy Papon, he was able to relate to me on my level without pretending because the child in him was very much alive. We played finger games in the seatless back of the car, made funny noises, and talked in silly voices. I remember how fascinating his skin was, different from mine and smoother than my father's, even my mother's. We'd settle down for a while, then start up again, two juvenile goofballs chortling our way happily across the plains.

Before showtime, after putting on his tap shoes, he got out a jumbo size jar of petroleum jelly, scooped out a gob, and put it on his hair. I later tried it myself and found it definitely kept my hair straight, although it didn't need to be. In cafés and truck stops, everyone looked at him from the moment he walked in with the unfamiliar stride of someone who makes a living with their feet. Many times, he was the only black man they'd ever seen in person. People gawked at how he cut his food, the way he chewed, how he swallowed. If he got up and walked to the men's room, every eye in the place followed him. Same when he returned to the table. At county fairs I was sometimes honored with the assignment of accompanying him across the track to the "donnicker" (carnie slang for toilets). No one told me it was for his protection from possible racial slurs at beer tents or from pugnacious teenagers that roamed the midway in packs. All those freaks with rubber skin, furred faces, and lobster claws were safely behind curtains, where you had to pay to see them—but Teddy, as another one of God's errors with his black skin and hair packed in Vaseline, was out in the open running loose and vulnerable.

Most of the time, however, he had to take his chances alone. Unlike his twin brother, he survived by getting laughs, yet he still had to go hungry from time to time because no café would serve him, and in addition he'd have to sleep in his car in the parking lot of the very place where he just knocked 'em outta their damn chairs.

But not all nights ended badly. After a few hours of heavy drinking, members of the audience might invite the black clown to join them. Sometimes he'd continue his wild tapdancing act in a nearby bar or even gather a crowd on the sidewalk. If some people can suck all the air out of a room, Mr. Rhythm, on certain occasions, could suck the air out of a whole *town*. On those nights he was the undisputed King and drank for free. But he knew, and so did everyone else, that by morning he'd better be gone.

HOUSE ON THE PRAIRIE

HALLOWEEN WORKS ESPECIALLY WELL for kids in trailer parks. With so many trailers packed in closely, trick-or-treating could yield a plentiful harvest. It was the only time that house kids, in disguise, ever walked freely in the trailer park, filling their bags faster than going from house to house. The smart ones started early, before the candy ran out. Not only did I start early, but I went around several times with different masks until I had more bags than we could fit in the trailer. Like all other excess, it went underneath, behind the wheels.

It was after Halloween that my mother received a tissue-thin letter in a nearly weightless envelope with a return address of Mahićno, Yugoslavia. It was written by someone named Janka Vrbančič. It sat for weeks with one of my mother's sisters who did not know who the woman was or how she got her address, or what the letter meant. It was passed on to another sister who also couldn't make any sense of it, then to my mother, who everyone thought was strange enough to find it interesting.

My Dear Cousin

I live her in Youglaera [Yugoslavia] we are Colica [Catholic] we are not comminisn we believe in God. And futher I would let you know that we have a poor life in this country and everything is very dear and we have high taxes in this country. The communish want us to go with them but we don't want to go for we are good Colica and we don't want to go with them. Dear Cousin my father is in Canadon [Canada?] in the city Hanalidon [illegible, Halifax?] and he does not ask for me. Dear Cousin I do wish if you could hep me with material and I could make my own clothes. Dear Cousin if you could send me a clock for I have no clock in my little home.

"Throw it away," my father said. "It's just another scheme to exploit American generosity. You send them a clock and they'll say it was broken and ask for another one. Next they'll want a coffee pot, then a typewriter, and then money for an appendix operation. It never ends. They don't know how to say thank you, either. Pretty soon you'll have Joe McCarthy coming after you."

As usual, she ignored him and sent cloth and a clock as requested to this Janka Vrbančič, whoever she was. My mother also enclosed a chatty letter about the magnet that had to be pried off a door with a crowbar, and how I went out on Halloween with different masks and collected more than my share of candy. She reported how they were cutting down trees to make room for more trailers. I don't know how any of that ever got translated, if at all, but over the next several months she received letters both in Croatian and tortured English from people named Josipa, Ignac, Franjo, Šimun, and Zdravko along with photos of grim-faced women and blank-faced children. They wrote, "times are poor," "the children are hungry," "we have no money," and asked, "where should we go but the street?" They referred to husbands who were "weak," "missing," or "haven't heard from." She didn't know any of them, nor did they seem to know who she was either, addressing her variously as Dear Cousin, Dear Auntie, Dear Bara (Barbara, her name), or Dear Ann (her sister's name).

"See what happens?" my father said. "They'll never go away."

It wasn't that he was indifferent to the suffering of others. I never saw him pass a beggar's cup without stuffing in folded money, especially if they played something sad on a musical instrument. He'd say, "There but for the grace of God go I," an echo of his youth in Baptist Rockport, where destiny was seen as preordained in a world of pitiless struggle. My mother thought beggars who played sad songs on the street were eugenic mistakes like the Human Pretzel, but she was moved by Croatian Catholics asking for fabric, shoes, crayons, aspirin, Band-Aids, toothbrushes, coffee, underwear, and mittens. She sent them everything they wanted, always enclosing a long letter and lots and lots of Halloween candy.

•••

MY FATHER WAS USED to knocking on the doors of farmhouses and asking for a plot of land to park the trailer on, but now he'd gone around asking if they had a plot of land to sell. Then it happened. He pointed to a place on a hilltop a mile away, beyond the swamps at the back of the trailer park. "It's up there." At that point it was only a "lot" known as "Registered Land Survey 11, tract E, subject easement." There was not even a road leading to it. We had to drive up Cemetery Road, then down Silver Lake Road to a place where surveyors had pounded stakes into the middle of an alfalfa field. It fell short on Cobbs' "Checklist For Choosing the Site," lacking "public transportation and convenient stores and schools," but was "free of excessive traffic and industrial smoke and odor." There was also "plenty of available play area" for me, even though no kids to play with. If I looked from the lot back down the hill toward the distant swamps, I could make out the tiny shape of trailers where there *were* plenty of kids to play with. When I looked along the horizon to the north, I saw a giant hill covered with many buildings and hundreds of lights, even in midday. The Arsenal.

After so many years confined to a car I was awed by the sprawling acreage that beckoned me with its slopes and small copses of oak and cottonwood trees. There was enough room to run at full speed in any direction. But none of this had anything to do with that other thing they called a "house." There was nothing inviting about that. It started when a bulldozer gouged out a huge hole in the field, leaving an open wound of clay and rock. In the trailer park I smelled the odor of trees freshly cut to make room for more trailers, and now I smelled the odor of earth excavated for the foundation of a three-bedroom shingle shake bungalow. The initial dig sat for weeks gathering water every time it rained.

Like ants making a hill one grain at a time, my father pulled cards from the air one at a time until he saved enough to buy a pallet of concrete blocks. Then more cards and a few bags of cement. Occasionally he hired a part-time handyman from the trailer park to help, but he was not satisfied with any of them. He was used to driving nonstop and portaging props across parking lots and up stairs until the job was done, then carrying it all back with no time to waste. His hired hands were slow and lazy, taking every opportunity to sit around and do nothing. Piece by piece, he amassed enough material to construct a basement and cover it with a floor.

Each step in the house's construction was separated by intervals so long I almost felt safe that this whole unsettling project would never be completed. Meanwhile, I relished my days playing with the kids of weapons makers but kept watch on that distant hilltop until the first signs of a house's skeleton were visible. When I walked through its open two-by-four frame, grasshoppers from the field landed on the wall studs, and the coo of mourning doves passed through nonexistent walls. I sensed the outline of a hallway and rooms, and one of them, they said, would be mine.

My father struggled with one hand or the other to wield a hammer and saw in constructing the house himself, one door and window frame at a time. He studied the Cobb book and tried to implement what he read, helped by diagrams from other sources and many trips to the lumberyard and hardware store. Like his own father, he did it without power tools, not because he rejected what was modern (as his father did), but because there was no electricity available to run them. He cut boards with a handsaw, the cuts deviating as much as a good quarter inch or more from the pencil mark. All this revealed a side to him I'd never seen before. His impeccable clothes became snagged and dirty. There was sawdust in his wavy hair. His fingers were wrapped in Band-Aids (removed at show time for painful and sometimes bloody card-producing). I could be with him in ways I never could when he was on stage or driving or sitting in the trailer practicing sleight of hand. I helped lift two-by-fours into place and hand up nails or a tape measure. Without my knowing it, I assisted in constructing, one nail and board at a time, a house of illusion.

A gabled, tarpaper box took shape in the middle of the field, an image as surreal as a newsstand on a desert. From the trailer park I saw it in the far distance up on the hill beyond the swamps. The house was considered complete when we could actually lock the doors, even though the windowpanes were not in the frames yet. By following Cobb's book, he did build it for less than $3,500. It looked normal enough, but on closer inspection everything about it was off. The floors weren't level, the beams weren't vertical, the joints misfit, and half the nails were pounded over sideways.

At this point it was an empty shell. It had to be brought to life with modern conveniences of the prosperous 1950s. My father had some knowledge of electrical wiring through his experience in the Seabees, so he bought several hundred feet of armored cable and drilled holes for it to pass through the studding and joists. He installed a fuse box and connected it to an entrance point outside. The nearest power line was at least a few acres away, so he had to persuade Northern States Power ("electricity is penny cheap") to run a line to the house and install a meter. NSP assumed other houses would eventually go up around ours and the field would become a subdivision (which it did), so they sent a survey crew out to determine where to put in electrical poles. After a long wait they pointed out that his wiring was in violation of the electrical code, so he had to hire an old electrician with a Norwegian accent to rewire the branch circuits, junction boxes, and outlets. I collected the circular slugs knocked out of the openings of what the electrician called the "yunction" (junction) boxes and kept them as imaginary pieces of eight like the kind I saw in the movie *Treasure Island*, which was shown at school for Christmas. While the old Norwegian wired the house in the proper way, he talked to himself as if he were another person telling him what to do, then while he did it he sang funny songs (*"when the ball was over she put in her old glass eye..."*). But the cost of his services was anything but funny to my father. It was quite the occasion, nonetheless, when we flipped the switch and light came from a single bare bulb in the empty kitchen.

The great schism finally occurred when we pulled our trailer from the prime spot next to the washroom and hauled it up the hill to the field where tire tracks had already worn a path. Its new parking place was behind the house, close enough to allow access back and forth. Many of my mother's clothes went directly inside and were hung from nails pounded in the wall studs. We had to carry water in jugs from a gas station, and because there was no longer a washroom, we continued using the bucket, except now we emptied it into a hole and threw in a shovelful of dirt.

I was a mile farther from New Brighton Elementary School, but there was a bus that picked up a few kids on Cemetery Road. I waited at the bus stop with three older girls and a boy their age named Bobby Cross who chatted away happily as if he were one of them. I decided to skip the bus and walk to school.

The real cost of this $3,500 wonder was yet to come in the form of modern conveniences that my father's parents regarded as making people soft and open to temptation. My mother was raised in a mansion, at least until she was sixteen, and after so many intervening years of privation, she looked forward to giving up the communal showers for a private bathtub, and that dreaded bucket for a flush toilet. She could not wait for her washing machine. Drilling for water became the first priority, and an expensive one. Because the house was on a hill, the drillers had to go especially deep. The cost was $1,373, according to the receipt my mother saved, more than a third the cost of the entire house and a huge expense for an entertainer making twenty dollars a performance before expenses. Finally, we had our running water (not yet heated, another frivolity) and a bathtub, but no sewage system. We could flush wastewater out on the field only so long. Paying someone to install a cesspool was too costly, so my father, bare-chested and wearing pants tailored by the incomparable Mr. Kuppleman, dug an eight-foot hole straight down through clay and rock. Rain turned it into a pit of mud that caked his torso and lacquered fingernails, but he persevered until the job was done.

Now my mother could have what she had dreamed of having for years: her very own bathroom complete with sink, tub, and flush toilet. Hot water and central heat were still a ways off. Compared to what she was used to, a toilet was the ultimate luxury, even though every flush could be heard gurgling its way through the shallow pipes and splashing into the covered cesspool. But it was better than carrying a bucket past a row of trailers to the washroom. Seepage from rainwater as well as sewage filled the cesspool faster than expected, so it had to be periodically pumped out onto the ground, but at least there was no one around to be bothered by the smell of open black water.

The house still did not have walls, so my mother tacked up sheets around the rooms for privacy. My father resolved to put up the interior walls himself. Each time he came back from an engagement he bought a few more panels of drywall. Now that there was electricity, he used a power drill to screw them into the studs. When I began to annoy him with my voices and repetitions, he suggested I busy myself by writing on the bare studs before they were walled in. I have no way of knowing what I wrote, short of ripping out the walls of what is now someone else's home, but it must have been similar to entries I made in other diaries at the time—which, of course, my mother saved.

> At school to day there was a big roll of papper. I moved it into the room. Then I moved it back. I watched Groucho they had a man with a turban.

Something like that. Maybe simpler.

Fortunately, the Prince of Pantomime happened to be passing through on the way to Kansas City from somewhere in the Dakotas. He was amazed at what my father had done by himself. On the promise of a place to stay in the future, he spent a day helping put up the ceiling panels, even though he had no more knowledge of what he was doing than my father. Together they were Laurel and Hardy, cutting sheets unevenly, bending and cracking them in the middle, miscalculating where to put the screws, and missing the studs. Billy's hair fell out of place and hung over his eyes, so my mother brought him one of her kerchiefs rolled up as a headband. As the walls went up, the empty house took on the heavy smell of gypsum. Professionals might have done it in a few hours, but it took them most of the day and into the night. Then they went into the trailer where my mother had the drop-leaf table set for supper. Billy took off the kerchief, and as we gathered around the food like nomads in a hut, a long strand of his incredible hair fell loose and hung down the side of his face all the way to his chin.

"How do you like the new house?" he asked me.

"I'd like it better if there were some kids I could play with."

"There will be, just wait. Once you have a house you are part of the community, not separated from it. You'll meet kids you'll know for the rest of your life." He turned to my father. "Think of yourself as landed gentry. Betty and I used to travel in a trailer, as you remember. She played accordion in the act and that was fine for a while, but then she wanted to live in a house and raise a family. I'm glad I did it. Sometimes it's a long drive back to Kansas City, but there were long drives with the trailer too. At least now I can travel a little faster. After we moved into the house, I joined the Old Mission Masonic Lodge. Harry Truman has been a member his whole life. I even met him once. Imagine, meeting the President of the United States. That wouldn't have happened if I was still pulling a trailer around the country. Now you can do the same thing. Become a Mason like me."

"I already am. When I was in the Marshall Islands during the War, I belonged to the Square and Compass Club."

"There you are. After I joined the Masons, I joined the Ararat Shrine and the Scottish Rite Bodies. It gives you a great sense of belonging. We visit other member's houses, and in the summer when I'm not working fairs I invite the members over for a barbecue in the backyard. Ruwe and Barbara come over too and sometimes he takes out one of his dummies for the kids."

"I'm not a joiner. I'm used to being on stage in front of people where I know what to do because I've done it before. When it's over I leave. If I'm in a group and try to fit in, everyone ignores me."

"It's not like that. The Masons, the Shriners, they're all based on fellowship and philanthropy. No one's going to ignore you. Good way to drum up a little business. Think about that."

"I don't know, Billy."

After we ate, my mother said, "You are welcome to stay the night, but I'm afraid we don't have a bed for you. But in the house, we can arrange some blankets on the floor and—"

"That's fine. I'll just drive home."

"You can sleep here any time," my father said. "Eventually we'll have an extra bed. You've put me up at your place often enough."

"See, there's advantages to having a house."

Outside the trailer, in the middle of a field with no streetlights, we stood under a vast canopy of stars. Billy pointed out two in the handle of the Big Dipper, one almost as invisible as a dressing room kid. He knew the names of both.

"See that star up there," he said. "The one that's kind of reddish? That's the planet Mars. If you had a telescope you could see canals all over the surface. Why else would they be there except that Martian people built them? If you looked down on the area around here from an airplane, you'd see lines all over the place too, roads like the ones your daddy and I travel on. These things don't build themselves."

Then he got in his dirty car, turned on the ignition, and made it come to life. I followed the taillights as it rocked over the rough path through the field and onto Silver Lake Road, then began an all-night, five-hundred-mile journey back to Kansas City.

•••

MY FATHER TROWELED JOINT compound over wide gaps in the sheetrock as if it were a silence over his life, then sanded down the whole crooked mess, entombing my thoughts scribbled on the beams. When the interior walls were up and the doors hung, my parents and I were now separated into private domains instead of living a few feet from each other as we did in the trailer.

After settling in our new home, unseen stresses from amateur construction caused it to groan in the wind as if in agony. There was little money for furniture and rugs to absorb sound, so the house had another strange quality—echoes. Every footstep, every handling of an object, every word reminded me I was living in a big empty place that never moved. Water, which had always been so hard to come by, was now the enemy. It leaked into the basement. It seeped through the eaves and soffits and stained the new walls. There were other invasions. Crickets found their way into the basement and chirped there. If my mother went down looking for them, they'd stop chirping and she couldn't find them. When she went back upstairs, they'd start chirping again. She sent my father down to get rid of them, but they stopped for him too. Jumping spiders hopped in sunbeams on the window ledges and centipedes got trapped in the bathtub where my mother picked them up with a piece of toilet paper and flushed them down the toilet. Others took their place. Salamanders moved into the window wells, frogs hopped above ground, and gophers burrowed underneath. The gophers especially bothered my mother, so she made my father attach a hose from the car's exhaust pipe into their tunnels to gas them. It didn't work.

Grover Ruwe was our first overnight guest. He parked his dirt-covered car at an awkward angle next to the house and stumbled out drunk. It was no surprise because he was that way much of the time. I knew that his dummies, whom he referred to in conversation as if they were real people, were in their cases in the trunk in a state of suspended animation. All entertainer's props had elements of sentience, but in Ruwe's case they had voices too.

Besides Louie, he had an old man dummy named Sunshine, constructed by the puppet-maker Ken Spencer. As Spencer aged, his eyesight deteriorated and the heads of his dummies got larger. By the time he built Sunshine, the dummy had a head bigger than Ruwe's. A wool beard covered the mouth area. For all the years

I saw Sunshine on stage, I never noticed until another ventriloquist pointed out, long after Ruwe's death, that Sunshine didn't have a mouth. The wool beard covered where it should have been. Maybe Spencer's eyesight was so far gone by then that constructing a mouth with moving parts was beyond his capabilities. Or, he might have given Ruwe a deal on a half-completed puppet. Another explanation could be that because Ruwe had no thumb and index finger on his right hand he was not able to work the mouth controls anyway. Compared to Sunshine, who had no lips to move, Ruwe's lips freely moved whenever the dummies talked. It didn't matter because all eyes went to them anyway and they were utterly, unbearably hilarious.

Instead of being cramped as we would have been in the trailer, we sat on folding chairs at a card table in an empty living room awash with the resonance of emptiness. My parents didn't drink, but for certain visitors like Ruwe, a bottle of spirits made its way out from some hidden place.

Like many ventriloquists, there was something darkly divided about Ruwe, as if his innocent eyes and fresh-looking face were a mask to some demon that came out only through his dummies, especially Sunshine, the grumpy (and dirty) old man. My father used to say, "Years of talking to a puppet has got to do something to a person's mind." He could respect Ruwe as a fellow entertainer, but he regarded ventriloquism itself as a developmental aberration similar to the way my mother saw contortionists. "They're all drinkers," he'd say, which was not entirely true. We also knew aerialists who drank—some rather heavily, like Karl Wallenda—but that didn't mean they all did.

Ruwe's mind may have been divided before he ever touched a puppet. His father taught at an auctioneer's school, and Ruwe started off in the same line of work but could not resist throwing his voice for nonexistent bids, something no one found amusing except him. His brochure advertised "Ruwe and Louie" as presenting "well-chosen material to fit every occasion." Louie was billed as "ad libbing with members of the audience, who always enjoy 'getting into the act.'" Virtually all 1950s performers, keeping with the times, emphasized how "clean" they were, but Ruwe never mentioned that. His brochure stated that his routine was "unusual in its freshness and originality" with sketches "especially appealing to children," but he was known to theatrical agents as a "stag act." Factories all across America had their own men's clubs that frequently booked exotic dancers as well as entertainers who could work "blue." Louie, the impertinent boy dummy, sat on one knee, and Sunshine, the old man, sat on the other. Sunshine counseled Louie on "the temptations of city life," a premise that could be an allegory for Ruwe's own life as a "blue room vent." If the hecklers got dirty, Louie and Sunshine got dirtier.

After his performances, Ruwe liked to bring Sunshine into a bar where the old mouthless puppet could be even more risqué than on stage. It was good advertising and sometimes led to another engagement. Even if he didn't get any business, at least he got free drinks. The more the highballs lined up in front of Sunshine, the funnier he got. And filthier. Sunshine did Lenny Bruce before Lenny Bruce, but from a bar stool—and without a mouth. A dummy can get away with more than a person, especially if operated by someone trying to restrain it, but in every bar there's always a hostile drunk who resents being insulted by a puppet. They think it's trying to prove it's smarter (which it is), and this creates a feeling of inferiority. And a need to lash out. I heard it said that Sunshine was once punched in the mouth he didn't even have.

In our bare living room, Ruwe poured himself a stiff one and said, "So I'm in Wellington, Kansas, doing a stag and they're all drunk. It's a dry county and they have to bring in their own booze. I'm out there with Louie and Sunshine and some pickled yokel starts choking on a maraschino cherry. Everyone thinks he's just laughing too hard but then he starts turning blue. A doctor comes over, drunker than the guy who's choking, pulls out a penknife and cuts a hole in his throat so he can breathe. Blood all over the place. Louie looks at the guy sputtering blood out his neck, then at Sunshine and says, 'What was that all about?' Sunshine says, 'Just a frog in his throat.' Then Louie says, 'I hope he doesn't *croak*!'

"Yeah," said my father, soberly. "I had a guy in the audience keel over and die on me once in French Lick. Fancy resort, big show. I didn't know about it until afterward. So how did the frog joke go over?"

"They were at the point where there was nothing they wouldn't laugh at. Dry counties, you know."

We fixed up a place on the floor for him to sleep like a homeless person in a doorway, and in the morning, he drove off to his next engagement, Louie and Sunshine in the trunk.

•••

THE TRAILER CONTINUED TO sit unlevel behind the house like some big abandoned thing, most of its contents having already migrated to closets and shelves inside. When my mother got a new stove and refrigerator, there was no longer a reason to be in the trailer. Every time I saw it out a back window it reminded me of a life far removed from what I was trying to adjust to. I went inside and tried to revive the feeling of what I once called home, but the smell of food and laundry and perfumed fur had disappeared as it reverted back to the impersonal odor of axle grease and wood laminate. The winter winds blew snow across the open field that drifted up against the side so I could not open the door. In spring, the drifts melted, and I could go inside again. On the shelves I saw only the memory of a lamp, radio, decks of cards, the plastic Fuller Brush letter opener, Skrip ink bottle, and dishtowel used as a movie screen.

When I walked across the field on my way home from school, my eyes always went first to the trailer as a sign of refuge. Then one day I looked across the field and saw only the house. It's still where my father built it, my scribblings sealed within its walls, and now part of a long-established neighborhood. The trailer could be anywhere. It could be crushed under tons of refuse in some landfill, now graded over and covered by tract homes. It could be sitting like so many trailers of its era, rusting in a junkyard or parked next to a farm shed with the windows broken and the inside taken over by swallows and raccoons. There is the wildest possibility it might still be a home to someone, maybe a child saying his or her first prayers in some ramshackle trailer park outside the limits of nowhere.

•••

SINCE ABSENT FRIENDS WERE the only ones my mother had, her written correspondence became voluminous. She received a great deal of mail from Croatia, which she always answered, sending whatever they asked for. If she needed a translation, she contacted people from the Croat community in Whiting, Indiana, where she was born. One of them was a nun who knew a relative in the Aršulić family, a grand-uncle's half niece, or something like that. In one of her letters the nun mentioned a "cousin Juraj" in Black River Falls, Wisconsin, not knowing it was the name of my mother's long-lost father. Taking a chance, she wrote a letter addressed simply, "George Arsulich, Black River Falls, Wisconsin." Someone at the Post Office apparently recognized the name because the letter was delivered and a reply came back. That's when her dramatic fits of crying became more frequent.

Dear Barbara,

The alld saying is still right that when you lest expect you sure get a surprise, received your letter and was very happy to here from you to know everything is O.K. you must have bin thinking of me laitly for you often came to my mind. Yes I have farm here but am not doing much just fucing around to keep myself occupied, I have no cattele only 30 pigs that's all. I was just thinking this morning of the day 47 years and 10 monts ago when a littele slim boy arrived from Europ to New York not knowing English lunguage but still brawe was not afraid even of devol who you soopose that was back in 1907 on fourth of July everybody was shooting fire crekers in solabration of new arrival from that littele Croatia. Hop this will find you and you family in good health an happiness best wishes to you from fogoten one.

Write soon Pop.

After the exchange of a few more letters she persuaded my father to drive her to Black River Falls to meet her father. He lived somewhere in a thick pine forest, and searching for his house got us lost on narrow, unpaved roads. We stopped at a small house nestled in some trees where my mother knocked on the door to ask directions. A man answered and spent a long time talking with her on his porch. I saw by their facial expressions the conversation was serious. He accompanied her back to the car and amid the thank-yous and goodbyes the man put in a last remark, "—and he was working on another one in Alma Center." The directions he provided took us down a dirt road to a clearing and a cabin next to a small field of corn.

The older man who came out to greet us bore a strong resemblance to my mother, and with the same animated outgoingness. He was dressed in a well-worn suit with wide lapels that made him look more like a sleazy car salesman than a farmer. They did not embrace or express more than cordial greetings, but as we moved to the inside of the cabin, I saw them throw assessing looks at each other.

We sat at a small table in the single room with a pot-bellied stove on a deeply warped floor. There was no furniture, no decoration, no television, nothing that would bring comfort to such a bleak interior. He seemed to have reverted back to the way he lived as an impoverished peasant in Varoš in 1907. In a primitive, wood-burning oven along the wall he had made a batch of ginger cookies. They were hard as rock.

"You got gray hairs!" he said to my father in a foreign accent. Juraj was twenty years older and had gray hair too, but not as many. My father clearly did not appreciate such familiarity from someone he didn't know. "I hear you are magician." Instead of the predictable comments about rabbits and hats he added, much more to the point, "You make any money?"

"A little."

"I see you drive nice car."

"It's my biggest business expense. I put on a lot of miles."

I sat through adult chitchat I neither understood nor cared about, but I do remember my grandfather going on at great length about some recent misunderstanding.

"All I said was I'm no fisherman. That's all. I'm no fisherman. And because of that they didn't want me to visit. Can you believe that? Just because I said I was no fisherman!" He smiled imploringly for sympathy, exactly the same way my mother did after telling her story about the blizzard. They had more in common than either of them realized. My father listened with the same impassive expression as when listening to my mother's woes. Grandpa Juraj seemed to me a little off, unbalanced. By the time we left I concluded he was more or less nuts.

During our brief visit there was no mention of why he might have disappeared in 1929 or what he'd been doing in the time since. He talked only of selling timber from a wooded area on his property and renting his land to someone to grow corn. And that he was no fisherman. Whatever emotion there was in the reunion remained unexpressed.

There were no more visits, but they exchanged letters, all of which, except the first, are gone—which is unusual, because my mother never threw anything away. Thereafter, Grandpa Juraj remembered me every Christmas with what he considered thoughtful presents of socks and underwear. They would have been a luxury in Croatia, but socks and underwear were not exactly what I wanted from Santa. Every year she made me go through the ordeal of pretending gratitude with a thank-you note.

•••

THE VACUUM OF EMPTY space inside our house drew in possessions to fill it. The smell of lumber, sheetrock, and paint was replaced by the smells of habitation: cooking, laundry, perfume, soap, ashtrays. The refrigerator held much more food than the icebox in the trailer, and to prepare it my mother filled the kitchen cabinets with cookware. We acquired furniture one piece at a time—first a dining room table, then a couch. Packages arrived from friends and relatives with items they'd been storing for her in their own basements and attics for years. The packages found their way into places yearning to be filled like an empty heart. Since no garbage truck came out to pick up trash, my father had to drive boxes of cans and bottles to the dump. The rest he burned. I stood next to him as he buried the ashes in the field as if they were the evidence of some awful crime. I could not help but remember where these burial sites were that seemed to contain more than the char of empty cereal boxes and old clothes.

To a traveling entertainer, having a house was more prestigious than a pinky ring or even dirt on the car. It meant success, or at least the appearance of it. My father took pride in inviting other traveling performers to drop in any time and stay the night to save a hotel bill. At our wind-shaken, water-stained bungalow, we hosted Rocky Mountain Mary ("Singer and Yodeler"), George Bink ("Comedy Juggler"), Jeanne James ("Exciting Acrobatic and Violin Stylist"),

Betty and Her Playmates ("cute and clever canines putting on the dog"), and, of course, the Prince of Pantomime and ventriloquist Grover Ruwe. If Teddy Qualls ("Mr. Rhythm") came by, we didn't have to worry about the racial judgments of neighbors, because we didn't have any. As long as I behaved myself, I could stay up with the adults and listen to everything that went wrong in their travels and on stage. I stared at them and studied their faces and listened to their every word, whether I understood what they were saying or not. It was also a chance to hear my father talk, something he seldom did otherwise.

It was always a special occasion when Billy Papon showed up, looking wasted and half-dead from the road, with dark patches under eyes sunk back into his skull and long strands of hair hanging down both sides of his face. All those hours of driving gave him time to think, and when he visited us, he was eager to share his thoughts.

"See this catsup bottle?" he said to me. "Someday it will be made of plastic. When that happens, you can fill it to the top, then with the bottom of each fist hit both sides and ketchup will shoot all the way up to the ceiling. That's how we'll put a man on the moon."

"How fast does ketchup travel upward?" I asked.

"That's an excellent question. A very excellent question. It's called science."

He removed some brochures from a briefcase and spread them out on our new dining table for my father to see. They were schematic drawings of an underground chamber that looked much like the inside of our trailer. One depicted the clip art figure of a smiling man in a suit and tie, smoking a pipe and sipping coffee, while his contented wife in a dress and apron read a book to her kids sitting on the floor.

"Bomb shelters," he said. "There's big money in it. What most people don't know is you can get blueprints like these free from the government. You build the walls a foot thick and if you want added protection you install a half inch of lead. For fresh air there's a blower, although radioactive dust isn't a problem, it's only the bigger particles you have to worry about."

My father glanced skeptically down at what was before him. "How do you run the blower?"

"Hand crank."

"Where's the toilet?" my mother asked.

"They've got these little bags. You wait a couple of days, then open the hatch door and pitch them out."

"I don't know, Billy," said my father.

"The real problem is this. Let's say they drop the Big One. You have a shelter. Your neighbors don't. You know what's going to happen? They're going to force their way into yours. You have a responsibility to your own family to persuade as many of your neighbors as possible to have a shelter of their own. I can build one for as little as two hundred bucks and then sell it for five hundred. The more the features, the more the cost. If people know it's for their own survival, they will gladly pay it. Think of the investment possibilities. The more capital I can raise, the more bomb shelters I can build, and the more profit there is for everyone. You must have some cash lying around you'd like to double or triple before Christmas. It could pay for a garage to your house."

"I don't have any cash, Billy."

"There's lots of ways to get capital. Think about it."

While my father was not thinking about it, I showed Billy the latest agates I found as well as the pods and seeds and insect husks, feathers, bones, and fur tufts from the surrounding fields that I kept in sparkling clean bottles with the labels soaked off. In the past these bottles of specimens would have gone under the trailer and left behind when we moved, but now they formed a permanent collection in the basement on shelves made from lumber leftover from the house.

A FEW WEEKS LATER Billy came through town again and contributed to my specimen shelves with samples of schröckingerite and uranophane, radioactive ores he picked up out west.

"They make A-bombs out of this stuff," he said.

Then he turned to my father with a different kind of news. "You can't believe how well I was doing with the bomb shelters. I built about a dozen. Things looked good. I had money coming in and had orders for a dozen more. The problem was, it rained. And when it rained, they flooded with water. I said I'd come out and install a drainage system, something they don't mention in the government blueprints. But I'm on the road a lot, and I can't get to things right away. You know how people are. They want everything now. It's not like nuclear war is going to break out in the meantime. A couple of people sued me, and I ended up having to refund everyone's money. Anyway, I've got a better idea. A much better idea. You're gonna love this one. With bomb shelters you have to go out to people's homes and present them with different plans and then send in a crew to dig the hole, bring in materials and so forth. And, I know, you have to put in a drainage system. But listen to this. You know the Russians have already put a couple of dogs into orbit, and they say they'll be landing on the moon in just a few years. We might even beat them to it. There could be gold up there. Uranium. It could be the biggest land rush of all time. You want to hear an idea better than money growing on trees? Selling land on the moon! It's all done on paper. Look how well Quaker Oats is doing selling square inches of land in Alaska."

"They have the Sergeant Preston show as a tie-in," said my father. "What have you got?"

"A plan to run ads in twenty newspapers. It's absolutely surefire. I already have people ready to invest. I was wondering if—"

"No, Billy. I don't have any money to invest."

"Not even a grand or two?"

"Not even a sawbuck or two. I just got a bill for the new dining room table and couch. It will take me a good ten or twenty shows just to pay for that."

Billy had to get back to Kansas City that night, so I went outside with him to his dirty car, where he directed my attention to the moon.

"Up there there's no seasons, no water, no freezing and thawing. If you dropped a marble it would stay where you dropped it forever. On Earth if you dropped a marble it would slowly sink and then rise up and then sink again as the ground freezes and thaws. Because they're round, they have no resistance to the surrounding soil and so over time they slowly bounce up and down. When I was digging bomb shelters, I found marbles five feet under the surface that were probably fifty or a hundred years old."

Unfortunately, the Prince's mind was on a different plane that everyone else's. Competitors in the fad took out competing ads selling not just acreage on the moon but entire stars, even galaxies, and then the craze died. He lost not only his money but the money of friends and relatives. He drank heavier than usual. As he stood at the microphone playing his harmonicas, alcohol on his breath gusted all the way to the front rows of the audience. Selling himself as the Prince of Pantomime, shaking hair over his face, and swallowing a tiny harmonica was the only enterprise of his that ever paid off.

WHO IS THERE

I NEVER GOT USED to the strangeness of living in the house my father labored so hard to build. When we lived in the trailer, I could stand in one place and reach almost everything I needed. Now everything was beyond reach. I had to walk across a room or down a hall. My bedroom had more square feet than our entire trailer and filled me with such agoraphobic dread that every night I clutched my stuffed Scottie, Sox, and struggled to fall asleep to the incessant monotony of tires humming over the pavement a mile away on Highway 100. There were knocks in the walls and what sounded like doors opening on their own. Heating ducts rattled like someone was trapped inside. Under the floor beneath my bed, instead of wheels, was that most dreaded of places: the basement, where intruders were waiting to get me. Above, instead of open sky beyond the ceiling, was another immensity called an attic that produced loud thumps. In the morning, sunlight poured through the living room window with more regularity than I was used to since the house always faced the same direction, and when I looked out across the hills covered with white in winter, green in summer, brown in fall, I saw in the distance the barely discernable trailers of Oak Grove Trailer Park.

Instead of taking walks with my father and pondering anthills, I went with him on long drives to Brown & Bigelow, the playing card manufacturer. Magic to me was not a matter of stardust and wonder, but a relationship with specific objects, usually hard to find. Because of moisture and handling and other factors in the world outside the sealed pack, he could not use playing cards more than once. He left every stage littered with them, so he bought them by the gross. Then he would dust a few decks carefully with zinc stearate (also hard to find) so they would slide more easily one over the other. The unopened packs went into his study, a newly created space that was exclusively his with a desk and typewriter. The room smelled like magic props: tannic acid, shellac, and damp silk.

On one of these trips I told him how I was always the last one picked when choosing sides for organized games on the playground. I knew it wasn't because I lacked strength or coordination but team spirit. Whatever my struggle, he advised me to take control and turn the tables. Life was a battle not to be won through confrontation, certainly not through coddling, but through cunning and manipulation, even lying if necessary.

"Start up your own game so kids come to you. Do palmistry using 'cold reading.' Palmists in carnivals use it all the time. You make general statements appear particular to give the illusion of clairvoyance. There's lots of ways to do it. You put something specific into a general question, like, 'Who is Mary?' They will search around in their head for someone by that name and tell you about her. Later they'll say, 'He knew all about Mary!' That's the way people think. They want to believe, and therefore they do. So after they tell you who Mary is, give details about her, using the letters of the name. M for money, A for angry, R for regret, and so forth."

"What does 'regret' mean?"

"Okay, use another word, something like 'return,' or 'rise.' Just remember to keep it vague so it could apply to anyone. They'll figure out a way to make it fit. Do it quickly, that's important. If you hesitate, it looks like you're not sure, and they'll see through it. The reason they want their fortune read in the first place is because *they* aren't sure. We all want to know our fate. Before a show I read the audience and try to figure out how they're going to react. Usually I can tell right away. But sometimes I'm dead wrong. When your mother and I were first married our future looked good. We played golf and canoed at Wisconsin Dells, and at night we went dancing. I said to myself I can't be any happier. But I was wrong about that too. After you were born everything changed. She became difficult and unreasonable and nothing could please her. Her sisters were the same way. When they lived at home, they screamed at each other, and when they got married, they screamed at their husbands. I told myself I would stay with her so you would have a father. Jerry grew up without one, and I didn't want that to happen to you."

That brought up many more questions, especially about Big Brother Jerry. Questions that would not be answered for many years to come.

On the playground I read a few palms, and sure enough, once the word got out everyone wanted me to read theirs too. I was surprised how little it mattered what I said and how easily someone could become so engrossed by looking into their own hand and believe something about themselves that was completely made up. It was like fishing for the first time and pulling them in. Then a few days later I found myself on the same playground with nothing more to offer, so the kids lost interest and returned to playing their own games, and I went back to running around with the outcasts.

•••

IN THE CLOSET TO my father's study was a trapdoor that led up to the attic, where all those thudding and thumping noises came from at night. Neither of my parents went there because it was too hard for them to stand on a ladder and hoist themselves through the opening, but I was young and limber enough scamper right up. In spite of its haunting qualities it became somewhat of a play area for me, a place to crawl around the rafters like a hovering spirit over the rooms below. When my mother was safely away, my father gave me a box of large brown envelopes and told me to take them up to the attic and push them back in a dark corner. It seemed a peculiar confidence, but I welcomed it as a shared closeness. The box remained up there unseen day by day, while down below I felt its unsettling presence. My mother had her own skills at divination, and they weren't fake. After a few card errands with my father, she took me aside and said, "I'd better not find out you're discussing things about me behind my back. I don't like secrecy, and I won't stand for it."

As if to offer me something my father could not, she brought me to places she knew would appeal to my sense of fascination. On weekends she took me to the Minneapolis Planetarium where I saw Billy Papon's universe mechanically rotating above me in the dark. At the Science Museum I saw dinosaur skeletons posed on platforms under lights like my father in Mr. Kuppleman's tailor shop. There were objects from the natural world illuminated in cases under spotlights like a Cavalcade of Attractions. She seemed to know that one visit to a museum would set off a lifetime of poring over anything shown in a glass cabinet, whether at a museum, a jewelry store, a shopping mall, or an airport. Perhaps my mother wanted my father to be a transparent cabinet too. On Sundays she brought me with her to Mass at St. John the Baptist Church, another kind of show, though considerably less inspiring than exhibits of reptiles and meteorites. Afterward she let me drop a couple of nickels into a slot and light two votive candles. She knelt and bowed her head, and I could tell by the distressed look on her face before the flickering flames that she was pleading for something in prayer.

THIRD ATTRACTION

ENTERING SOCIETY

I BECAME LESS AWARE of the envelopes in the attic by the time my father went on an extended USO tour of radar installations along the Distant Early Warning Line (DEW Line) constructed in the arctic as a defense against a Russian sneak attack over the North Pole. The military flew him to these remote locations, so he didn't need his big Oldsmobile, which my mother was grateful to have available for trips to the store and St. John's to light votive candles. Since moving out of the trailer and into a house with indoor plumbing and places to put things, she had to give up something in exchange. She no longer had her laundry room society and no audience for her home movies. Instead, she spent her time in solitude writing stacks of letters to people she had met on our travels. At a gas station, a check-out line, or a laundry room, she might sweep others into her private confusion, but at the same time she would not abandon them afterward. I still have one of her large address books full of names and endless changes of address for people all over the country, with additional return addresses torn from envelopes and stuck between the pages in as chaotic a manner as the circumstances under which they were first acquired. She even wrote letters to me, leaving them on the dining room table so I'd find them in the morning before I went to school. But the days of my writing her back with I-love-yous and big Xs were about to be over because an unwanted guest arrived that could neither be ignored nor gotten rid of.

Pubescence. With startling suddenness, internal secretions pillaged my gangly body. It was nothing less than an all-consuming debacle. The repeating thoughts that had plagued me since child-hood went completely out of control, and my mother, so much in need of human contact, had to put up with my parroted lyrics from "Short Fat Fanny" and "Great Balls of Fire" and every sort of stray phrase in endless profusion. If called upon to answer a question in class, my voice broke like a skin of shattered ice. I cleared my throat so aggressively that my teacher thought I was doing it just to get attention.

All the things I used to do, from standing on my hands, to juggling clods, to reading palms no longer got me the attention I sought. It seemed that everyone around me spoke a different language. Cliques and hierarchies made no allowance for someone used to packing up and leaving town the next day. I carefully observed those who fit in and tried to imitate them, but the results were disastrous. It was little comfort that I was not the only outcast. The massive giraffe of a girl named Muriel Grosvenor had a growth spurt way ahead of everyone else's. She liked to push boys into a corner and stare at them as if something miraculous would happen. She targeted me too, and I must admit that although I was just as much of a social failure as she was, I joined the mob in heaping ridicule upon her because we were all in the same hell of Hobbesian meanness.

The boys in my grade could be divided into two distinct groups, those who managed puberty and those, like me, who did not. Those who did not, like Gaylen T. Patterson (he always introduced himself with the middle initial), Darryl Wegehaupt, Scott Mechtenberg, and Dean Pashold roamed the student body as serial goosers, urinal shovers, and erection advertisers. They were the very types of outsiders who always welcomed me as one of their own.

Because the War delayed my birth, pubescence unfortunately coincided with my mother's menopause. She had episodes of being too hot, and on the coldest winter days turned the thermostat down to fifty degrees and opened the windows. Her moods were more erratic than usual and she burst into tears more often. The few houses that began to be built around ours were spaced an acre apart and the housewives were all much younger with babies. She might have had more in common with them ten years earlier. There was no common place to meet, like a washroom, so they remained isolated in their bungalows. She was shut up with me. Whenever I brought home one of the few odd friends I managed to make in faraway neighborhoods, she scrutinized them for faults. Jim Olshevsky, who lived two miles away and went to parochial school, was thirteen but already starting to shave. To her a child with an Adam's apple and whiskers was just as repulsive as a human pretzel. He loaned me some hot rod magazines and when she found them said "souped-up cars are for delinquents" and threw them out. Then she forbade me to see him anymore.

But I did anyway, in secret.

I continued to associate with Edgewood Junior High's phratry of hormonal train wrecks. Gaylen T. Patterson, with his glasses and alert manner, was the only one who provisionally passed my mother's scrutiny. In class he raised his hand when no one else did, even though he often had the wrong answer, but knew it would ingratiate him to his teachers. Behind this façade of the eager student lurked a shocking array of foul behaviors. He ran his fingernail down the zippers on the backs of girls' dresses so it felt like they were being unzipped and relished their shocked reaction. He brought a copy of *Peyton Place* to school and read the juicy parts out loud. He was always eager to thrust his hips forward and show the bulge in his pants to anyone who was interested. Even if they weren't interested, he'd show them anyway. Somewhere he acquired a black-and-white pornographic photo in the form of a playing card. It was a blurred close-up of two people in copula that he tried to explain, but my knowledge of sexual anatomy went no further than the cheesecake calendars on the wall of the Texaco station where my father took his car for servicing.

•••

AT MY BUS STOP, Bobby Cross finally began to notice me outside his closed circle of girlfriends. His lips were dark, almost like he wore lipstick, and his hair was always perfect. He sat in the back of the bus and laughed and chattered with such animation that kids taunted, "You sound just like a girl!" He was not interested in roughhousing on the playground, but we did have polite conversations while strolling down Cemetery Road. When I brought him to our house, my mother took me aside and told me, "I don't want to see that boy here ever again."

"Why not?"

"He's a fairy."

"What's a fairy?"

"Someone with a glandular problem."

I didn't know what a glandular problem was even though I had one myself and so did my mother. Like the other boys she disapproved of, I saw him in secret too.

Most of the girls in my class were repulsed by the smuttiness of my friends, but there were a few who relished it. Kristine Lane was a flat-chested acne case who eagerly joined in the ribaldry. Baxter, a rough-featured girl known only by her last name, was possessed of a husky voice and explosive horselaugh easily brought on by anything obscene. It was reassuring to know we could always get a rise out of her. All of us lived for disruption, so Gaylen made a crude sketch of a phallus and wrote the word "cock" with an arrow pointing to it in case it wasn't clear enough. When the classroom was most serene, I slipped it over to her. She slowly unfolded the paper with great anticipation. Then came the inevitable.

Elmwood Junior High made an enlightened effort to deal with all the hormonal changes going on within its walls. In health class we cracked up over diagrams of ovaries and testes, and in gym class there were frank tutorials on pubic hair, but there was careful avoidance of any direct reference to what was foremost in everyone's mind: sex.

That was supposed to be taken care of in the home, but it never was.

In a noble attempt to promote healthy interaction between boys and girls, Edgewood held dances during the last hour of the day. Kristine Lane, Baxter, and, of course, Muriel Grosvenor were not afraid to cross the no-man's-land of an empty dance floor and pull some boy out of his seat to dance, but the more alluring girls kept to themselves and waited for the ordeal to end so they could go home and talk on the phone with their older boyfriends in high school. Sitting in the middle of them, completely at ease, trilling away happily, was Bobby Cross.

Most students dealt bravely with the challenge of dancing with the opposite sex, but there were those who turned the floor into an interactive disaster of forced belching, gas passing, and free-style scrotum assault. Teacher-chaperones took this all in stride and tolerated the buffoonery as a necessary step to maturity, but in the classroom stricter order had to prevail.

Mrs. Grolisch, my English teacher, would have been proud, even amazed at the influence she had on the dastardly dingbat of a magician's son she must have thought was one of her least promising students. Unknown to her, and even myself, she aroused within me a deep appreciation of literature. I was never interested in books for young readers, but through her I immediately came to know and appreciate Coleridge, Twain, Poe, Hawthorne, and Dickens. Being awestruck can render someone speechless and speechlessness can sometimes be mistaken for ignorance. I saw why the pumpkin trick worked so well in the Sleepy Hollow story since I was familiar with the nature of sudden appearances, but explaining it out loud was beyond my capabilities at the time. I found that certain lines and phrases ("eftsoons his hand dropped he" or "the melancholy House of Usher") played into my predilection for repetitive thought and replaced the lyrics to "Tutti Frutti" "Flying Purple People Eater." No comfort to my mother.

The incident that subverted all this occurred the moment Mrs. Grolisch was trying to teach the concept of metaphor. I understood what she was saying, although I would not have been able to explain it in my own words, especially to other students who didn't get it at all—some of whom were brazen enough to ask why it should even be worth learning. But she was young and enthusiastic and took up the challenge, slowly reciting from Joyce Kilmer: "I think that I shall never see / A poem as lovely as a tree," then allowing us to savor the meaning. Not much savoring took place. As she repeated it a second time, Gaylen, sitting across from me, got my attention by thrusting up his hips to show off a bulge as if he had a tree inside the front of his pants. I clamped my hand over my mouth to hold back the laughter. Baxter saw it too, and we both could hardly contain ourselves. Emboldened by our reaction, he thrust his pelvis up again, and I threw a sharpened pencil at the fabric stretched tightly over the bulge. It stuck momentarily like a dart before falling to the floor. Gaylen let out a muffled oomph and doubled over. A loud burst from Baxter set off the whole class. I didn't realize it at first, but Mrs. Grolisch had seen the whole incident. She abruptly left the room, which immediately fell to disorder, and a few minutes later Gaylen and I heard our names over the intercom summoning us to the office.

Mr. Helstrom, the principal, was a man in his forties, very tall, nearly a giant, with a deep voice and a serious manner. He was omnipresent in the building—at the front door when the buses arrived, in the halls, the lunchroom, the library. It was as if there were fifty Mr. Helstroms throughout the building keeping an eye on everything and everyone at once.

"Do you know how completely fed up I am with all the bad reports I'm getting on you two? Mrs. Grolisch is a dedicated teacher. She says this is the sort of thing that makes her want to quit teaching."

I suddenly saw a similarity between teaching metaphor to a couple of seventh-grade dolts and pulling cards out of the air for drunks. I remembered how devastated my father was by an unappreciative audience. Here I was, one myself. I was at a loss for words. Or even a single word.

"I'm calling your parents to come in for a conference. Maybe we can get to the bottom of this behavior you've been showing so you can better spend your time learning."

When I got home my mother was furious. She'd had all day to let Mr. Helstrom's phone call grow in her mind and plan a crusade of correction. She gave me a booklet from the vestibule at St. John's Church titled *My Body Is Changing*, published by the Catholic Family Press.

"Go to your room and don't come out until you've read it. Cover to cover. *Twice*."

"What is it?"

"You'll see. Just read it. Every word, all the way to the end."

"I'll do it later."

"No, you'll do it now."

So I dragged myself to my room and tried to make sense of all the vague references to "urges" and "fluids" and "temptation" and "self-abuse."

"Okay, I read it."

"Are you sure? You didn't give it much time. Is there anything you didn't understand?"

"I guess."

"What?"

"All of it."

"That damn father of yours is the one who should be here explaining it to you."

That night she took me to St. John's rectory to have a talk with another father, Father George, one of two priests at the parish. She must have chosen Father George because of the sermons he gave about teenagers and sin. He was greatly bothered by all the heathens at Mounds View High who walked past the church's elementary school every day, setting a bad example with their cigarettes, leather jackets, and ducktail haircuts. During one Sunday sermon he bitterly denounced a girl who lost her faith after she started dating a beatnik. Her parents wanted to rescue her, but "they couldn't go where the beatniks go." He was especially harsh on sins of the hair. Dye jobs, wearing it too long, combing it in public. I could only imagine what he would think of the Prince of Pantomime. In one of his sermons he mentioned the time he went into the church lavatory after a funeral and came upon two boys in front of the mirror. He held an extraordinarily long pause as everyone waited for what he was going to say next.

"They had peroxided their hair!"

Gasps came from the congregation. I had to ask Gaylen what "peroxided" meant, but he didn't know either. I finally found out from Kristine Lane.

Father George's office was dim with a single lamp on his desk casting shadows over his full-moon face. After one of his trademark pauses, he said, "Your mother tells me you're doing things a Catholic boy shouldn't do. And by the way, why are you going to public school when we have a perfectly fine seventh grade here at St. John's?"

"Edgewood has a science department."

"Science? What's so special about that? I suppose, since you go to public school, you've forgotten the commandments. Do you remember the sixth one?"

"Thou shalt not commit adultery."

"That's good. I hope you continue remembering it. Do you know what it means?"

All I gleaned from the *Baltimore Catechism* my mother made me memorize for confirmation was that it meant no thoughts or actions having anything to do with sex.

"Sex outside of marriage can get you into a lot of trouble with the Lord. Are you married to this..." He shuffled among some notes. "Gaylord Peterson?"

I gave him the obvious answer. He was intensely curious about exactly what Gaylen and I did and how many times we did it, but I was as embarrassed to go into detail with him as I would have been with my father. When he didn't hear what he wanted to hear, he went into a grisly story of how Saint Bartholomew was skinned alive. Then he elaborated on all the tortures inflicted on Catholic missionaries by Godless Indians whose morals were as corrupt as mine and "Gaylord Peterson."

"They heated metal hatchets until they were red hot then wedged them in the buttocks of the very priests who tried to save their souls. You know what the Communists did to American soldiers in Korea? They shoved chopsticks into their sex organs. You know what they did then?" Long pause to imagine the worst. "They broke them!"

He went on like this for an hour with the strategy of mortifying my impure thoughts, then asked if I wanted to make a confession. My mother had gotten me to believe in heaven and the sacraments, and absurd as it sounds, I can say there was somewhat of a pious side to me. But I was not about to confess my shameful secrets to a dour priest sitting across from me at a desk. All I wanted was to get out of there as quickly as possible. To his annoyance I said no, I did not want to make a confession. He gave me his blessing anyway. In Latin. As I left, he looked at me in disgust. As if I'd peroxided my hair.

•••

WHEN MY FATHER RETURNED from the North Pole and heard about the conference he was supposed to have with Mr. Helstrom, there was more than the usual dissension in the house. Everything unsaid was deafening. When the day came, my mother arrived in furs and costume jewelry and my father wore one of Mr. Kuppleman's suits along with dazzling cufflinks. He smiled his broadest stage smile and my mother turned on her best charm. This was a performance to show Mr. Helstrom that they were of a higher "class" than, say, people from a trailer park.

He asked my father what he did for a living and his answer followed the usual pattern. "I'm in show business."

Which led to, "Oh, really? And what do you do?"

"I'm a magician."

Then the incredulous smile and, "With the circus?"

Which led to the required correction, "I just completed a USO tour in Greenland, Iceland, and Newfoundland, and all along the DEW Line."

At this juncture there would be one of two reactions. Either indifference, because not everyone is impressed by such a thing, or free association into clichés about rabbits and hats.

"Do you pull a rabbit out of a hat?"

"I use a rabbit in a gag with silk handkerchiefs. I couldn't bring it into Iceland so once I got to Keflavik Air Base, I tried to find one locally. What I didn't know was that there are no rabbits in Iceland. There are none in the wild, and they won't let any into the country because if they escape they multiply and take over the puffin nests. I thought of using a baby sheep, but it was too big. As a last resort I used a stuffed fox, but it didn't get the reaction I wanted. Once we got to Nunavut Territory one of the installation officers got me an Arctic hare from a biological station. They told me it had been handled since birth and was tame, but when I produced the thing it went berserk and hopped all over the Nissen hut. They opened a door to chase it out but all that did was lose all the heat from the room. Outside it was seventy-five below. The band covered me with Keystone Kops music while the whole audience tried to catch the hare as it jumped over tables and bounced off the walls. Once we got to the DEW Line, they dispatched a Fairchild C-119 to fly in a white New Zealand doe from a medical lab in Fairbanks. The plane was designed to transport entire tanks and airplanes but when they opened the cargo bay there was only this small cardboard box with a rabbit huddled in a bed of shredded newspaper. I used it for the rest of the tour. Before I returned home, I gave it to some Eskimos on Baffin Island. I think they ate it."

Both my parents excelled at presenting themselves publicly and so they managed to make an impression on Mr. Helstrom that rescued them, and me, from deeper embarrassment. If we could move on to the next town as we'd always done, a situation like this would have been left behind and forgotten, but it was the price we paid for giving up the nomadic life and living in a house. The meeting ended with agreement that all I needed was more to challenge my mind, so I joined the Service Club, setting up projectors for classroom films. That provided perfect cover for me and my priapic friends to snigger among ourselves in the dark.

•••

MY FATHER NEVER BROUGHT up the incident in Mrs. Grolisch's classroom or used it as a basis for one of his allegorical stories about entrapment. Unlike Father George at St. John's, he didn't want to know any details. I was grateful that he spared me that embarrassment, although I would have probably clammed up like I did with the priest. Or lied. He was as content as I was to leave everything unspoken and buried, whereas my mother would not let either of us forget it.

He stayed away for longer periods—by car—and when he returned, she berated him for leaving her "stranded in a field to raise a troublesome boy." Since she couldn't pick on him when he was gone, she picked on me instead—especially if I showed any sign of secretiveness. If I came home later than usual after listening to Bobby Cross's Perry Como records in his bedroom, she demanded to know where I'd been. Since I wasn't supposed to associate with a fairy, I made something up, but she knew I was lying. Eventually my father's dirty Oldsmobile reappeared. After weeks of isolation in a creaking and groaning house with a filthy-minded liar of a son, she unleashed her wrath upon him over everything from using too much jelly on his toast, to trimming his mustache hairs over the soap dish.

Our trips to Brown & Bigalow for more playing cards became important occasions for both of us. We took solace in each other's silent company. I didn't know what his thoughts were any more than he knew mine. When he did speak it was to say something momentous, a something made all the more momentous by his actually saying it. "Your mother is very unhappy living where she is. What would you think about moving to Milwaukee? We can build another house there, a better one, and she would be near her relatives and old friends. It would be convenient for me because Chicago is only eighty miles away and that's where a lot of my business is shifting."

The idea of living in a new place went over well with my mother and took her mind off of her grievances with my father and me. They settled on the Milwaukee suburb of Brookfield with its long-established subdivisions of houses on curved streets with quaint names and large, tree-shrouded estates built before the War. It had evolved into a community of such quiet permanence that it was difficult to find an available lot, but they did find one on the slope of Pilgrim Road next to a row of box elder trees.

Instead of sawing and pounding the house together himself, he hired contractors, but things went no more smoothly than last time. He had blueprints drawn up that my mother rejected. He hired architects who quit in exasperation. She demanded a walk-in garage, floor-to-ceiling picture windows in a cantilevered living room, and a huge fireplace large enough to roast an entire magician. One idea, from which he could not dissuade her, was to have large, double-pane windows installed in the basement. This involved specially designed window wells. After years of tubs and ringers in trailer parks and the dank dungeon of the New Brighton house, she wanted to enjoy sun pouring in while she did laundry in the popular image of the smiling housewife in a frilly apron. All of it required pulling an enormous number of cards from an enormous amount of air.

After five years in the New Brighton house, the longest we ever stayed in one place, I did not have a single real friend, with the possible exception of Bobby Cross. But he had his own group of friends, older boys I didn't know—even adult men I'd see driving him around. Everyone else lived too far away to visit except by special arrangement. I was alone most of the time, but at least I wasn't as bad off as poor Muriel Grosvenor, whose doorway ambushes and unwelcome notes and gifts to boys brought her such ridicule that she was always crying in class. In the middle of the school year her parents took her out of Edgewood and put her in a private school.

Every time I passed through the living room, I looked out the picture window across the rolling hills to Oak Grove Trailer Park, where my old playmates had long since receded into the past. Hidden in that landscape between the trailer park and the Arsenal were many houses, and within those houses lived boys and girls my age, but having them as friends was not as easy as knocking on their door and asking for them to come out. Adolescence involved more complicated maneuvering between acceptance and rejection. I longed to run with a crowd of real teenagers, but my only friends turned out to be people in books. Little did Mrs. Grolisch know that because of her I was reading Jules Verne, H. G. Wells, Jack London, and Daniel Defoe. They spoke to me in a way that books for young adults did not. They picked up where my father left off with his cautionary stories. In Verne's *Journey to the Center of the Earth,* Prof. Lidenbrock was Billy Papon, showing me an entire ocean below what was mere surface to everyone else. *The Time Machine* brought me to a place that seemed quite familiar: a society consisting entirely of giant crabs. When Bobby Cross and I took our walks down Cemetery Road and along a tree-shaded creek, I'd set down my *Robinson Crusoe* next to his book with a cover illustration of girls looking over their shoulders at boys in the distance, and we'd linger next to a trickle of water and try to figure each other out.

TEMPTATION

AT THE BEGINNING OF grandstand show season in Montana and Wyoming, construction started on the Brookfield house. The plan was to move out of the prairie house at the end of summer and start a new life in another city, and I would begin high school and associate with friends from respectable suburban families. The county fair circuit that year was booked by the Clarence Smith Agency out of Salt Lake City. It was a typical grandstand production with a stage across the track and large backdrop panels of scenery propped up with braces. The truck that carried the scenery panels and spotlights was backed up to one side of the stage and doubled as a dressing room. The musician's instruments were stored in the truck every night and carried from town to town. As usual, the wind blew over the scenery on a regular basis and the stagehands would scramble to set it back up while the band kept playing and the show continued. At teardown, the bent nails were always saved in coffee cans for set-up at the next town.

On the lineup that year were two newlywed acrobats glowing with love but on the borderline of being too old to perform. There was also a musical trio called the Harmonicats, a family of trampolinists from Britain, and an animal act consisting of a loquacious trainer and three trained chimps transported in small cages that would never pass animal rights scrutiny today. At unexpected times, sometimes during the show itself, the chimps would start up a round of hoots loud enough to be heard all the way outside the limits of the fairgrounds.

Smith had hired not one but two puppeteers by mistake, and so he decided to use one of them with the odd name of Air Metz, while the other traveled with the show and did nothing. I saw them in a bar one time sitting silently side by side on adjacent bar stools. Before the other puppeteer went away, he sold Air Metz one of his marionettes that did a striptease. The audience loved it, especially when the tasseled breasts bounced up and down on strings, but Smith was an elder in the Mormon Church and did not approve of unclothed puppets, so he made Metz take it out of the act. Instead he used three hillbilly marionettes that sang "Cigarettes, Whiskey, and Wild, Wild Women." Even though it was a song condemning vice, Smith didn't like what it referred to. But he let it pass.

Even though my father was middle-aged, gray-haired, and walking with greater difficulty, he still had the agility to perform the Trunk Escape. He locked my mother inside a box and laced it around all six sides with a canvas cover while the orchestra played "Hindustan" at double tempo. To do this he had to set the microphone aside but continue a running patter, projecting his powerful voice across the racetrack to the back rows of the grandstand. As he finished lacing up the canvas, making escape look impossible, he made the same joke he had made for all the years he and my mother did the trick.

"We've been married twenty years. Seems like only yesterday. But you know what a lousy day yesterday was!"

The audience laughed, but the joke was really for the ears of eternity.

He stood on the box holding a curtain, then ducked down and my mother's head popped up. She instantly dropped the curtain and he was gone. Disappeared. She unlaced the canvas and unlocked the locks and there he was inside the box where she had been. They came forward holding hands and took their bows, smiles gleaming in the spotlight. Night after night, from Lewiston to Miles city, from Glendive to Sidney, they were the ideal of glamour, the very image suggested by the words "show business." But deep, unseen cracks widened behind the image. There was so much tension between them offstage that I preferred to sleep in a pup tent near the rodeo arenas rather than stay in a hotel room with them. Sometimes my father parked the car behind the stage and slept there while my mother stayed alone in the hotel. During the day he watched rodeo clowns butted over corrals by Brahma bulls, and she struggled with her dust and dander allergies at blue ribbon jam and flower exhibits. I went off by myself looking for moss agates in dry streambeds.

There were other problems too. The chimpanzee trainer bothered some of the other performers with his tasteless jokes and they began to find him as obnoxious as the hooting chimps in his truck. The bass player with the Harmonicats, a high school senior, suddenly announced he was leaving the tour early to start football practice. Smith was furious because posters showed a trio and he was afraid the fair managers would complain if one were missing. It was decided I should wear the bass player's wardrobe (much too big for me) and pretend to play bass so it still looked like a trio. Then there were problems with the British trampoline act, which consisted of a heavyset older man, his wife and daughter, and another woman with long, unshaved hair on her legs that showed in the stage lights through her fishnet stockings. He complained that the band wasn't playing his stage music correctly and was throwing off their stunts. Then he made a big deal out of someone supposedly peeking in the dressing truck while the women were changing. My father warned me not to go anywhere near them or the dressing truck. One night a fair manager wanted to make an announcement after the show, as they commonly did, mostly to hear themselves talk.

"We're working hard to bring you the best," he said to the crowd that ignored him as they exited the grandstand. "Next year we're going to bring you an even *better* fair with an even *bigger* carnival, and a bigger grandstand show with even *better* entertainment that will…"

At that point the trampoline patriarch rushed to the microphone and muscled the fair manager out of the way.

"What do you mean *better entertainment?* We've performed all over the world in London, Paris, Berlin!"

Smith and my father tried to pull him away, but he wouldn't go. "We once performed for the Queen! The *Queen!* You can't get any better than that!"

Smith and my father finally pulled the trampolinist away from the microphone and the skirmish continued backstage, where they tried without success to cool things down. The trampolinist tried to recruit bystanders into his tirade but no one was willing to step in. With nothing resolved, the fair manager went away bewildered. As stagehands struck down the scenery, I overheard people say the manager was indeed a fool, but the trampolinist should have known that Smith made a living—as they all did—by keeping such fools happy.

The scenery went into the truck along with the band instruments, and the performers either went to their hotels or into sleeping bags under the stage or the grandstand. I went to my pup tent near the rodeo stalls. With nothing but the sound of grazing livestock—and a few intoxicated cowboys—I read the adventures of Odysseus by flashlight.

•••

IMMEDIATELY AFTER THE LAST show on the circuit, instead of finding rest, we drove all night nonstop back to Minneapolis. My father planned to rent a cargo trailer and haul a load of furniture and other essentials to the new house and get me enrolled in school. When we arrived at the house in the field, my mother threw out all the food that had spoiled in the refrigerator and lamented over her garden gone to weeds. There was no time to sleep. We began loading the cargo trailer. Just as we were about to leave, he called the contractor in Milwaukee about getting a key and found that the house was nowhere near ready. Water and electricity had not been hooked up. My mother said she refused to use a bucket for a toilet again and bury the contents in the yard, especially when surrounded by new, affluent neighbors. My father and I unloaded the cargo trailer and put back the furniture. He and I would go ahead to Milwaukee without my mother and do whatever was necessary so I could at least start school. I did not need the pup tent but brought along my sleeping bag.

Before we left, my father took me aside and said, "You know that box in the attic? The one with the envelopes?"

It had been so long I had almost forgotten it was still there.

"Bring it down and put it in the trunk of the car. Lay something on top so your mother can't see what it is."

We drove all night and arrived at our unfinished house late the next morning. He made sure I put on a white shirt and tie, then dropped me off at Brookfield High School to enroll myself while he went to unload the car. This was the way it had always been. Each of us had things to do that did not involve the other. I went to the office and presented myself, unregistered and not assigned to any classes, which had already begun a week before. I had no transcripts from Edgewood Junior High, no gym uniform, no locker, no paper or anything to write with. My previous surprise arrivals had been in small town elementary schools that had autonomy and flexibility in such matters, but this was a large suburban high school and things were different. The principal, vice principal, and several secretaries gathered around the counter to try and make sense out of me.

"Where did you say you lived?"

I took out the piece of paper where I'd jotted down my new address on Pilgrim Road, even though there was no finished house, no telephone, no mailbox. They passed the paper around as if looking at it might explain something.

"Tell us again why you're a week late starting classes."

"I was with my parents in Montana and Wyoming."

"On vacation?"

"No, business."

"What kind of business?"

If I said my father sold insurance I would not have had to explain more. But I'd be at this school more than a few days and they would eventually find out. I said, "Grandstand shows at fairs."

"He's with the carnival?"

"He has nothing to do with carnivals."

"You just mentioned sideshows at fairs."

"*Grandstand* shows. That's different from sideshows."

Whatever the meaningless distinction, they could not send me out the door into truancy, so for the moment they had me fill out some preliminary forms and make a quick choice of subjects for the semester: civics, English, algebra, Latin, biology, and physical education. Then the vice principal escorted me to Miss Haller's English class, which was already in session. Her whole body, including her face, looked like it was pumped full of tallow. She and the vice principal went out in the hall and remained there a long time. Meanwhile, everyone stared at me. Even though I'd been through this experience many times, I was now thirteen and horribly self-conscious. I felt my ears get hot and knew they were turning red. If I put my hands up to cool them down it would only draw more attention to them, which was why they were red in the first place.

Finally, Miss Haller returned to the room and arranged some papers the vice principal had given her. She seemed to be as curious as everyone else about who I was and why I showed up late, so, deciding I was too obvious a distraction to be left unnoticed, she announced my name to the class and asked me to say a few words about myself. There went my ears again.

I tried to explain that my father was a magician who performed during the summer at grandstand shows.

"What a coincidence," said Miss Haller. I noticed she had a peculiar diction as if the tallow had infused its way into her tongue. "I'm writing a book about a magician. It's a romance..."

A couple of boys laughed mockingly as if they couldn't reconcile her doughy figure and puffy face with anything romantic. The laughter seemed especially cruel at her vulnerable moment, but she ignored both it and me as she smiled and transported herself into distant thoughts.

Brookfield Central was such a spread-out building I got lost trying to find my way to other classes. I walked in late each time and had to answer the same question, *Who are you and why are you late?* At the end of the day I took an armload of textbooks and tried unsuccessfully to find my locker somewhere in a complex of hundreds of other identical lockers. So I carried them all with me. Buses were lined up to take everyone home, but no bus arrangements had yet been made for me. With an intuition that comes from being in strange places, I found Pilgrim Road and started walking. Reckoning from the sun's position (as I'd learned from Billy Papon), I headed north with a stack of books that grew heavier the longer I carried them. Students on passing buses looked at me as they passed, some laughing. After a couple of miles, I came to the house where my father was sleeping in the car. I didn't ask him about his pressing matters, and he didn't ask about mine. Inside the empty house, his unsettling box of envelopes sat out in the middle of the floor.

"I have to leave for Chicago," he said. "Since you'll be at school all day you can use the bathroom there. Otherwise, figure something out. I laid in an assortment of canned goods and a box of candles so you can have light. Somewhere I packed a can opener and some plates. The contractor left a ladder in the basement. Before I go, put that box of envelopes in the attic for me. Put them way back in the corner like you did at the last house, and, good God, don't mention it to your mother."

"How will I cook?" I asked, staring at the box.

"Pretend you're a cowboy. Make a fire in the fireplace. Be sure to open the flue or the whole house will fill up with smoke." I had no previous experience with fireplaces, so he had to show me how to do it. For writing materials, he gave me some Master of Deception stationery and a flat carpenter's pencil. Then, as he had always done, he got in his car and drove away.

I gathered up enough box elder branches at the edge of the lot to start a fire in the fireplace and fashioned a way to heat a couple of cans. I spread out my sleeping bag on the floor and began catching up on my assignments, working into the evening by candlelight. The next morning I lugged my load of books down the street and joined a group of other students waiting for the bus. When I tried to get on, the driver said I needed a pass, which I didn't have, so I walked to school, shifting the books from arm to arm and was an hour late without a note from home. They couldn't call my father because we didn't have a phone yet, and besides, he was in Chicago trying to figure out a way to pay for the house. After someone helped me find my locker, I used the lunch money my father gave me to buy a bus pass. In a few days he returned from Chicago with fresh provisions and arranged for the electricity to be hooked up so I could cook on a hot plate and do my homework on the floor by lamplight.

"I just talked to Billy Papon in Kansas City," he said as we ate our first hot meal of canned stew in the house together. "He said Ruwe was in a bad car accident. He's in a coma, and it doesn't look like he's going to make it. I knew all that drinking and driving would catch up with him sooner or later. It shows what can happen when you don't have self-control." This was followed by a lot of chewing in very long silence.

One would expect my sympathies to go to Ruwe's wife and son, but for some reason I thought of his dummies, Louie and Sunshine. What would become of them? His wife and son could take care of themselves, but what about those inanimate creatures in his trunk who had no life without him? As dummies, they faced an indifferent world alone. Self-reliance did not apply to them.

•••

As IN OTHER SCHOOLS I attended, I wasn't the only outcast, and soon enough I befriended a fat, freckle-faced sophomore named Craig Tyler who rode the same bus. When he wasn't shunned, he was picked on. Students would rather stand than sit next to him. There was hardly an upperclassman who did not go out of his way to bump into him or flick him on the ear. Like me, he resigned himself to his role and tried not to show that it bothered him. It turned out we had somewhat similar backgrounds. His father, who died the previous year, used to work for the Milwaukee Braves baseball team. Before that it was the Red Sox. Craig grew up in locker rooms and dugouts just as I'd grown up in dressing rooms and hotel lobbies. His father was not a ball player but worked in some job behind the scenes and was known by the nickname "Milky Way." He was on the cover of a magazine that I remember as *Look* or *Life* framed on the wall of their living room, but I have not been able to find the same cover on any issue of either magazine from that time period. Nor have I been able to find any reference to a "Milky Way" in the archives of the

Braves or the Red Sox. But Craig (and his mother) knew so many details about the baseball business and famous players that I'm sure it was all true.

Although Milky Way was not famous enough to have left a historical record (that I can find), he must have made a good living, judging from the large ranch-style rambler he provided for his family, even though it had fallen into a state of decay. When Craig invited me there for the first time, I smelled spoiled food and dirty laundry piled up on the elegant furniture. The thick carpeting near the doors was flattened with dirt and mud. Every surface was covered with unopened mail, solidified half sandwiches, pencil stubs, overflowing ashtrays, and empty cigarette packs. His mother was bleach blonde, tall, and imposing with a ski jump nose that gave her face the look of a snowplow. She swooped through the house with an ever-present glass of sherry and a retinue of fruit flies.

He had two younger sisters. The older one was in the eighth grade and chubby like Craig. The youngest sister, about six, was thin and usually sat on a pile of old laundry rocking back and forth sucking her thumb. She had asthma.

He brought me into his pigsty of a room as his mother yelled after him with a Boston accent, "Clean up your room, Craig! Do it now!"

"Go to hell," he said with a laugh, slamming the door.

He showed me paperbacks with gruesome cover illustrations of soldiers in hand-to-hand combat and read some awful passages aloud while his mother pounded on his door, yelling, "Bahstid! Craig, you're a dirty bahstid!"

I wondered what things were like when the grinning man on the magazine cover was still alive.

•••

WHEN THE WATER WAS hooked up and the plumbing fixtures installed, my father left me alone and drove back to Minneapolis to pick up my mother. They returned with a rental trailer full of furniture. This was a new beginning, right? No more trailers without a bathroom, no more house that creaked and groaned in a field every time the wind blew, right? We were supposed to be happy, right?

Nothing changed.

When my father was home, which was not often, she barely spoke to him and, if she did, it was in the coldest tone. If he was there for dinner, he ate as if it were prison food, his brow furrowed in a look of gloom.

She had better hopes for me. In one of her high school yearbooks retrieved from years of storage in someone's attic, she showed me photos of herself in all kinds of school activities from debate team to golf league. She said that's what I should do too, enrich myself by associating with other well-adjusted, obedient teenagers. When the phone was hooked up she talked with her old classmates who had teenagers of their own, all good students active in wholesome activities. Esther Zivnuska's son got all A's and had a part in the school play. Nora Norquist's daughter went on a trip to Washington, DC, for a National Student Council Convention. But none of those wholesome achievers were raised in a dressing room.

THE FALL

M Y FATHER TOOK ME aside in his study where I noticed a ladder leaned against the wall. "Your mother's coming up with all kinds of suspicions. Wait until she leaves the house to go to the store, then bring down that box of envelopes before she gets her hands on it."

Now the envelopes were more than unsettling. They were ominous. Too ominous to ask about. I was sure that box contained more than business papers. I grew up with the assumption that backstage you controlled your curiosity about what was going on, because it would interfere with the sanctified focus on everyone's performance. Each had some kind of gaff to what they did, but you never asked about it any more than you dared to touch their props. To me this was still backstage, and I knew to keep my mouth shut.

The show must go on, and so I waited. If my mother went to the store it was when I was at school and when I returned, she dogged me around the house. If I went anywhere near my father's study she was there too, pretending to be doing something else. All three of us knew there was something in that attic, though it was out of reach to everyone but me.

My mother was pleased that I began to show a new enthusiasm for accompanying her to Mass at St. Dominic's. When I put on my best clothes and carefully combed my hair on Sunday morning, she thought I was doing it for God. But I was not. I was doing it for Karen Kiedrowski, an eighth grader I sometimes saw walking her dog along the curved subdivision roads near our house. She went to Sacred Heart Holy Angels, an all-girls academy in Milwaukee where she was an outcast too. Her brother had died of kidney failure about the same time as Craig's father, so she and Craig became friends on the basis of family tragedy. Her manner was quiet, almost pious. She had stunning platinum hair and a big nose. In church she sat with her gruff, bear-like father (with an even bigger nose) on one side and her older sister and mother on the other. Craig told me, "Her father won't let her have anything to do with boys. If you call her on the phone and he answers he'll just hang up on you. But she has her ways. I go see her sometimes when she babysits."

Since I appeared to be turning into a good Catholic boy, my mother let me sit wherever I wanted in church, which was as close to Karen as possible. Then I watched her recite all the proper responses in Latin with her head bowed in devotion, angelic hair modestly curtaining her face.

One Sunday after church I went to Craig's house where his mother had nothing but kind words for me because I attended Mass and studied Latin in school. She hugged me in a boozy fog and give me a kiss on the cheek and told me what a good boy I was, unlike "that bahstid Craig." He brought me into the sanctuary of his room while his mother ranted outside the door.

"Take a look at this," he said, handing me a tightly folded sheet of notebook paper. "It's from Karen. She and Patricia wrote it together. Funnier'n hell."

Patricia was another eighth grader who also sat with her devout family at Mass in St. Dominic's. She was one of the few friends Karen was allowed to have. Their note began "Dear Craigie" then started off by flatly saying that "we," meaning Karen and Pat, were "going to take off all your clothes." That was provocative enough, but they went on to say they were going to tease him "to make it hard." Nothing about him doing anything to them. Then came the "funny part," requiring a shift to the first person singular. "I'm going to give you a blowjob and spit it back in a French kiss." I already knew what a French kiss was, but to show how little I knew on the cusp of the 1950s, I had to ask Craig the definition of "blowjob." Oh, yes, that. I remember Gaylen T. Patterson mentioning something of the sort but couldn't imagine someone actually doing it. It had to be one of those purely imaginary things. I was amazed at how these two apparently devout Catholic girls, both still in grade school, came to be so practiced in raw whore talk. That new word immediately took on repetitive qualities in my mind along with the image of Karen's angelic hair curtaining her bowed head. The strangest part to me was Craig's indifference to the whole matter. He found his cheap paperbacks on war and atrocity far more interesting. Maybe it was this indifference that made Karen and Patricia want to have a little fun with him. Or they knew it would get to me and I would react with anything but indifference.

"You going to write her back?" I asked.

"I don't know. Probably not."

I returned home with the words *Dear Craigie, Dear Craigie, Dear Craigie* repeating in my mind. In my bedroom I opened my algebra book and pondered which of the two girls came up with the idea for the note and who did the actual writing. What were they expecting by way of response? My mother always made sure I wrote a thank-you note to Grandpa Juraj for the socks and underwear he sent me for Christmas, and to anyone else who wrote or gave me anything. Craig could not put two sentences together if he spent all day, so I took it upon myself to show Karen and Patricia the proper courtesy. Just as I was beginning to give it my best effort my mother came in with fresh laundry to put in my dresser. I scrambled to cover what I was writing.

"What are you working on?" She leaned over to have a look.

"Nothing," I said. "Just an assignment for Miss Haller."

"May I see it?" She reached down to pick up what I was writing. Then suddenly we heard a loud crash from my father's study. She rushed out of my room and I stuffed the note in my textbook and followed her. We found him sprawled on the floor next to a box and a scattered bunch of brown envelopes. One foot was swollen and turning purple. He looked helpless, not because of his injury, but because the contents of his secret box were out in the open and there was nothing he could do about it. Apparently, he had decided to go up to the attic on his own while she was occupied with me in my room. He must have come up with the strength to climb through the trapdoor, but I knew from experience that getting back down was the hardest part. He'd apparently misjudged his footing and fell. My mother and I helped him to the car, but once he was seated and immobile, instead of taking him to the doctor, she went back in the house and gathered up the envelopes in a bag and brought them along. *Then* she drove him to the doctor. While a cast was put on his broken foot, she examined the envelopes in the waiting room.

She did not share the contents with me, not that I even wanted to know, but it seems to have been largely about money, like my Croatian grandfather's suitcase full of "concealed assets." When a husband thinks marital collapse is imminent, he would want to pocket as much of their joint assests as possible, and his wife likewise. Apparently, it had gotten to that point. But there might have been more.

That night, when I was supposed to be asleep, I heard her wrathful voice outside my door, using words like "secret," "deception," and "lies."

"All this time you could have afforded to buy me a car, you cheapskate!"

He mumbled something I couldn't understand.

"Oh, don't give me that nonsense!"

Then there was the sound of scuffling.

"Stop kicking my crutches! You're going to make me fall again!"

"You made yourself fall, you miser!"

There was more scuffling, then my father's voice pleading. "My glasses! Don't step on my glasses!"

I heard a crunch.

"I'd like to step on your head, you snake!"

Within me a voice kept repeating, *Dear Craigie, Dear Craigie, Dear Craigie...*

•••

THE AMERICAN GUILD OF Variety Artists had originally offered to compensate him twenty dollars a week in disability for as long as his foot was in the cast, but that was not enough to live on, much less pay for a new house. He came up with the outlandish idea of continuing to perform by wearing a peg leg so he would have both hands free to pick pockets and shake a rabbit in someone's face. His proposal was that if AGVA paid for the peg leg he would forfeit his entitlement to the twenty dollars a week in disability. When they agreed to the deal, he went to a prosthesis shop and had them tool a peg leg from a single piece of wood, then paint it matte black. The design was based on the leg used by Peg Leg Bates, the tap dancer, who knelt into the device with a shaft extending up the hip to a strap around the waist. Unlike Bates, who actually did not have a leg, my father's lower extremity stuck out the back with a cast on the foot. It looked ridiculous and I almost laughed when I saw it, but his grim scowl told me it was not a laughing matter.

On October 10, 1961, his picture appeared in the *Milwaukee Journal* leaning back in a chair with his foot encased in plaster and propped up on a table. Next to it is a top hat with cards strewn about. He holds a huge peacock fan of cards like the one in his Tenkai photo, but instead of a smile he wears an expression more miserable than the one I was used to seeing at the dinner table. The headline reads, "Tumble 'Grounds' Flying Magician."

"We flew thousands and thousands of miles, and then I came home and broke my heel in a four-foot fall!"

That's the story Magician Jack Pyle, 3760 Pilgrim Rd., Brookfield, relates these days as he entertains Milwaukee area groups as he did servicemen at Strategic Air Command bases at the North Pole.

Along with a four-piece combo band, Pyle and three other acts—including two girl dancers and a female singer—visited SAC bases in Iceland, Greenland, Newfoundland and the ice cap bases around Thule.

"The girls were especially welcome at the outposts around the magnetic North Pole," Pyle recalled Saturday as he sat with his foot propped on a table. He said during their 11 week tour, "Some of the planes were in pretty bad shape. In fact, one crashed on the flight after ours and all aboard were killed."

Returning home, Pyle went into his garage to store some props. He climbed up a step-ladder which suddenly began to spread, causing him to fall. "That's how I broke my heel," he explained.

My mother waved the newspaper in his face. "You weren't putting away props, you liar! And where did the 'girl dancers' and the 'female singer' come from? You said there were no women on the tour. Did you think I would never find out?"

"I was at the Press Club with that crazy Burmek and he's trying to get me a booking. That's what he does. He's an agent. Someone asked about my foot. You know how he is when he starts drinking. He came up with a story idea. Flying magician falls. They set the whole thing up with the top hat and the cards. You can't go by anything he says."

"I can't go by anything *you* say. You were hiding your whole life from me. I found the contract. That USO tour ended two weeks sooner than you said it did. So which one of the 'especially welcome girls' were you with for two weeks?"

She called the reporter and told him every last detail of why my father was in the attic (not the garage, as stated in the article), plus some extra tidbits of her own. He was not "putting away some props" but engaging in a marital deception. She demanded they print the truth. The reporter said that human interest fillers were simply not important enough to retract. They were printed merely for entertainment and to take up space on the page. She went to the editorial offices and tried to speak to one of the editors. After that the secretaries were instructed to screen her out. The crying never ended.

The story did not get me any attention at school. In fact, it was barely noticed. Only Miss Haller and a couple of students asked, "Was that your father in the *Journal*?"

When I answered yes, nothing more was said.

•••

ONCE HE MOVED OUT, large items started appearing like cards from the air: a new refrigerator, a dining table, a bedroom set, all the things my mother felt she had been deprived of. The next time his name appeared in the *Milwaukee Journal* it was in a classified ad stating, "I am no longer responsible for my wife's debts." It didn't matter. Things kept coming. I came home from school to find a 1958 Chevrolet Impala parked in the driveway so she could drive to the store or St. Dominic's. The people at banquets for Edison Electric, Motorola, Cyanamid of Canada, and American United Life Insurance had no idea where the "debonair man of mystery" came from or where he went after he entertained them. They didn't know that his home was a new (dirt-covered) Buick LeSabre with the engine running to keep warm.

She hired a lawyer who advised her to contact every agent and performer we ever worked with, from Sophie Tucker to the Daring Lavodis, every trailer park manager and babysitter, and ask them to write a deposition stating that he deprived her of food and sleep, locked her in a box as entertainment for others, paid her nothing, and hid the proceeds. Late into the night I heard her typing letters to fairground managers, fraternal club presidents, and AGVA offices, but her requests led nowhere because most of the time, even if she located the people at all, they didn't remember who he was. His momentary acts of amusement months or years prior were no more significant than a sip of water. She hired detectives to dig up dirt on his out-of-town activities, but his life was so diffuse he was impossible to trace. It was money wasted. Her grounds for divorce included mental cruelty and adultery, neither of which could be proved. She accused him of everything from tax evasion to conspiring with Big Brother Jerry to fly in contraband from the Far East, all without proof. Furthermore, he was a bad influence on me. His lawyer wrote briefs alleging she was unstable and delusional, a matter equally evasive of solid proof.

MAGICIAN JACK PYLE, HIS PROPS AND INJURED FOOT

Tumble 'Grounds' Flying Magician

"We flew thousands and thousands of miles, and then I came home and broke my... visited SAC bases in Panama, Puerto Rico, Iceland, Greenland, Newfoundland and the ice...

weeks ago, Pyle went into his garage several days later to store some props. He climbed up a step-ladder which suddenly began to spread, causing him to fall. "That's how I broke my heel," he explained.

In the middle of all this was the unfortunate incident with Karen's father. While snooping in her bedroom he found my thank-you note and was so shocked by it that he called the police. "Not even in the army," he told them, "did I read anything that filthy." He saw Craig's name signed at the bottom, and knew he was the fat boy whose father just died.

Captain Richard C. Grammons of the Brookfield Police took on the case. He was in his fifties, heavyset, gray hair, and his face was a fierce wall of brick. Underneath the tough exterior was an avuncular gentleness that might have been why he was police captain in a bedroom community like Brookfield and not some urban precinct with a murder rate. If someone hopped the fence at the Victory Drive-In or put a cherry bomb in a mailbox, he'd sleuth out who did it and pay a visit to the perpetrator's house. He started off playing bad cop, opening his suit coat to reveal his gun and badge, then grab the trembling culprit by the shirt and pull him right up to his bifocals. He softened up at that point and played good cop with a lecture on citizenship, then turned control back over to the parents, who were grateful for his intervention. That was usually enough.

Grammons went to Craig's house and demanded to see a sample of his handwriting. Of course it did not match. Craig said he had no idea who would write such a thing. But the captain knew how to crack a case. Further inquiries led to the knowledge that Craig's only friend was me. He drove his unmarked car to our house where he showed his badge to my mother and said he was investigating a complaint.

"May I please see a sample of your son's handwriting?"

She was all too willing to produce something I wrote for Miss Haller's class. One look and Captain Grammons knew he had his man. Two big fists grabbed me by the shirt and pushed me up against the wall.

"Do you know you could go to jail on a moral's charge for writing something like that? Where did you learn such filth?"

That was a question without an easy answer.

"It wasn't from me," said my mother. "Talk to his father."

"And where might I find the father?"

"Who knows. We're separated."

"Where does he work?"

"He's in show business. It could be anywhere."

"Was he the one in the paper with a broken foot?"

"That's the bastard. But don't believe a word of what he says. He's a big liar."

"Does he have visitation rights?"

"Whenever he feels like it, which isn't very often."

"Next time he comes around to see the boy, I want the both of them to come down at the station."

That idea pleased my mother greatly.

The captain gave me a parting lecture on citizenship, then drove away.

When word got back to Karen and Patricia that the police were involved, they were terrified I might turn snitch, but with the honor of one outcast to another, I assured them their virtue would be preserved. I dreaded each day that went by—and there were quite a few—until my father exercised his visitation rights and picked me up in his LeSabre covered with a fresh layer of dirt. I opened the door and smelled the familiar rabbit pee and hair oil. He moved the detached peg leg to the back seat to make room for me and drove away with no destination in mind. I stammered out the story of my poor citizenship and how I was supposed to bring him to the police station for a talk with Captain Grammons. Now we had a destination.

My father was not angry. In fact, it seemed like he already knew what it was all about. When we entered the station with its tacked-up notices and wanted posters, all activity stopped. Eyes turned to the somber-looking man in the expensive suit lurching his way to the captain's office on a custom-made peg leg even though he was not missing either leg. He shook hands with Grammons as if he were the client at an engagement then labored himself awkwardly down onto the chair. The cop and the conjurer looked at each other a long time. As my father changed position, the peg leg, where it fastened to his belt, made a creaking sound. Grammons leaned forward in his swivel chair and its leather seat made a similar creaking sound.

"I read about you in the *Journal*," Grammons said. And then the old cliché, "Do you pull rabbits out of hats?"

"Mine comes out of the air."

"Out of the air?" Grammons snapped his fingers. "Like that?" His mirth was not infectious. "Do you know Peter Hurkos, 'the man with the X-ray mind'? He lives here in Brookfield. Supposedly he's solved twenty murders."

"I've only seen him on TV."

"They say he can see what's sealed inside an envelope."

"He's never done it in front of me, so I don't know."

"He makes a good living at it, that's for sure."

"Apparently. First he worms his way into cases that aren't going well and offers to help for free. What's there to lose? He dreams up this and that and most of the time he's wrong, but sooner or later he's right just by the law of averages, so he publicizes it for all it's worth. Pretty soon everyone's calling him and he's no longer working for free."

Grammons considered this at some length. "I'm not a psychic, but it's my job to look into people's minds and try to figure out what they're up to. Like your son here. We responded to a complaint on October fourteenth by Walter Kiedrowski alleging that his thirteen-year-old daughter had received an obscene letter signed with the name Craig Tyler, a fifteen-year-year old with whom your son associates on a regular basis. Here is the letter and here is a page of schoolwork written by your son that his mother provided. I would like to draw your attention to the contents of the letter as well as the handwriting."

My father looked at the letter long enough to get an idea what it said then set it back gently on the Captain's desk as if it were a performance agreement.

"The reason I called you here is because I'm concerned about what's going on in the home. The boy's mother alleges you are legally separated from her and in your absence he is unmanageable. She says he has put salt in her coffee and stubbed one of her cigarettes in her oatmeal. She says he stands on his hands on the dining room table and juggles eggs, which he sometimes drops. So far, he's had no other run-ins with the law, but you understand that if we get a call, we have to respond to it. If we feel action needs to be taken, by statute we have to take it. If the incident falls under certain criteria, we are required either to make an arrest or refer the case to another authority."

My father tried to defend me by saying my mother was emotionally unstable, but the captain ignored that. There was another long pause while they tried to read each other through their bifocals.

"Ten times Herkos is wrong," said the Captain. "And no one notices. The one time he's right, everyone notices. Interesting. Ten times your son is a good citizen and everything is fine. Then the one time he slips up, bang, he's in trouble. For the moment he can get away with it because he's a minor. Here's the situation. The girl who received the obscene note is also underage. If your son were, say, eighteen, we'd have no choice but to file a charge. That could follow him around for the rest of his life."

There were a few more exchanges between them ending with a promise from me to practice restraint in the use of my pen. As we made our way out of the police station all activity stopped once again, and everyone stared at the grim Long John Silver in a bespoke suit lurching along on a peg leg attached to a fully intact leg.

•••

AT THE NEXT CUSTODY hearing I was ordered into the judge's chambers. I took a seat. Hunched forward in black robes, the judge squinted at me through layers of cigarette smoke with eyes draped in folds of sagging skin. Next to a giant overflowing ashtray and a high stack of files and papers, I saw my note to Karen. He picked it up, and I watched him read the words I had written for eyes other than his. He had the mordant manner of someone who had seen it all and heard it all before and was inured to a daily grind involving everything that did not illuminate the soul.

"You wrote this?"

I had to admit that I did.

He looked at it some more, as if it were a document that required the closest examination.

"Are you aware that what you have written here is illegal under present law?"

I said that all I tried to do was write a thank-you note and got a little carried away.

He leaned forward, his robes spreading like the wings of a giant crow. "Some thank-you note."

That was all he had to say before granting custody to my mother.

With a malice peculiar to unmanageable adolescents, I baited her with insinuations that more or less reflected what my father's lawyers were alleging in court, and this set off tirades where she withdrew all privileges until further notice, which was pointless since I'd learned from Craig that I could ignore her and do whatever I wanted. If I left the house without permission, she called the Brookfield police to pick me up and bring me back. Squad cars became a familiar sight in the driveway, which did not help her desperately sought acceptance by the neighbors, but it did elevate my status with other defiant teenagers who saw me on display in squad cars as if I were a real juvenile delinquent. Neighbors shunned her, partly because of me and partly because of the stigma of being a divorced woman. Having nothing better to do, the cops drove me around and told me about their time in the military and advised me to hang on until I turned eighteen then join the army. I kept them company on their boring patrols through subdivisions, responding to calls of people locked out of their houses and prowlers that were never there.

Seeking companionship, my mother joined the Holy Rosary Society at St. Dominic's. All she did was talk about how horrible it was being married to a magician who locked her in a box and abandoned her to die in a blizzard. They gave her insufficient sympathy. Looking for anyone who would listen, she joined the Brookfield chapter of the John Birch Society. At first the middle-aged crackpots welcomed her to their small weekly coffee sessions in someone's living room where they bonded through a shared fear of communism. Their current project was trying to remove a social studies teacher from Brookfield High because he once worked for the State Department and therefore had to be a Communist. But what my mother wanted to talk about was outside their scope of interest; she didn't last long at the John Birch Society, either.

•••

CUSTODY WENT BACK AND forth between my parents depending on the judge. The ones who wore the robes in their chambers usually gave custody to her, and the ones who didn't gave custody to him. As legal and other bills began to mount, the house had to be hastily sold at a loss. So much for permanence. All three of us returned to being as transient as when we lived in the trailer, except now it was each of us separately. It often became a shell game with none of us ever quite sure where the other was. I don't know how we managed to locate each other, but we always did.

My mother was taken in by a number of rescuers. At first, she slept on the couch of an elderly woman she met while volunteering at a nursing home. The woman's husband had just died and she appreciated the company, but not the anti-magician rants. Next was a Baptist minister and his family. They had no idea that taking her into their house also meant taking in a generous load of boxes filled with pamphlets for every attraction from the Canadian Rockies to the Sonoran flatlands, trailer park rental slips, newspaper clippings going back to the 1930s, stereo photos of me with playmates whose names I'd long forgotten in towns with names I never knew, film reels of small parades and carnival lights at dusk in anonymous places, and five- and ten-second snippets of all the things people pay to be amused by. And the bullfight. And the blizzard. With characteristic assertiveness she worked her way into activities at his church, organizing progressive suppers for teens and scavenger hunts for kids. Friction arose over her being a Catholic getting too involved in Baptist activities, so she moved everything into the home of a Jewish couple she met through a mutual friend. A mountain of boxes sat in their living room while her hosts stood to the side, perplexed by what their generosity had gotten them into.

As she found it ever more difficult to recruit movers, her possessions went back into the basements and garages of people she had not seen since the War. Some had already cached her treasures for years while we traveled in the trailer and now found themselves caching them again. Even though she might have had legal custody of me that month, in all the confusion over moving I took the opportunity to run away and stay in a motel or rooming house with my father. When he was out of town, I skipped school and hitchhiked downtown to see a movie, read in the library, browse at the Renaissance Bookstore, or go to the weight room at the YMCA and engage in the solitary struggle of lifting dead iron against the inexorable pull of gravity. I fell behind in class assignments, but I caught up by using memory systems well known to magicians, amateur and professional, and used by my father to memorize a weekly *Saturday Evening Post* as part of his act. It's an ancient technique of exaggerated association, the biggest trick being simply to implement it. It did not make me an A student, but it did get me passing grades and made my teachers curious as to why I retained information by page number.

Compared to the empty suburbs, the city was teeming with activity. There were people everywhere, many more than kids in trailer parks. Some were elegant, like my parents tried to be, and others were street degenerates, more interesting because they were outcasts I could identify with. I marveled at all the raw truths before me: flattened circles of gum that had become part of the pavement like so many polka dots, each from a mouth with its own story to tell, and dropped hankies, nice ones. I saw highball glasses that managed to migrate to the curb, where there was sometimes a splotch of blood. I watched a ragged man mumble to himself as he rummaged through litterbins, taking out scraps of paper, which he wrote on, then threw back. When I dug in one of the bins after him to see what he was writing, I found it was only squiggles. Because of the War? At the central library I discovered authors I'd never find in a school library: Andre Gide, D. H. Lawrence, Violette Leduc, Henry Miller. I don't know how I first got to know their names, but like outcasts everywhere, we met eventually.

Out of concern for my immortal soul in all this turbulence my mother enrolled me in what turned out to be a series of parochial schools. Truancy was the biggest problem, as well as bringing to class books from the Renaissance Book Store that were on the *Index librorum prohibitorum*, like *Hunchback of Notre-Dame*, *Candide*, *The Red and the Black*, and *The Immoralist*. I wrote theme papers on disturbing topics like sway poles and ventriloquism.

•••

WITHOUT MY MOTHER TO lock in a box, my father substituted her with what magician's call "close-up," going from table to table at banquets, either before or after the stage presentation, to conjure up close. With the decline of the floor show, this was an emerging novelty and my father was one of the first to exploit it commercially. Most people welcomed his presence, but it was not uncommon for them to say, "We'd rather you leave us alone," whereupon he politely excused himself and went to another table.

When I was old enough to get a driver's license, I helped with driving, which meant further absence from school. I would probably have skipped anyway, something he knew about and tolerated since my grades were generally good, but if I was driving, at least he knew where I was. I became useful in another way, too, as a secret part of his act collaborating in a bold deception. While holding forth at a banquet table with people standing around watching, he'd catch my eye, then discretely show me the bottom card in the deck. If it was, say, the three of spades, I'd whisper to the person always on my right (his left), "When he asks you to name a card, say the three of spades." Then I'd walk away. After a side steal of the three of spades, he made a seemingly casual adjustment to the tablecloth in front of him while slipping the card underneath and ruffling the cloth so it rode a current of air down the table a good six feet. He'd say, "Anyone, name a card. Anyone." As if at random he indicated the person I'd told.

Not always, but most of the time the person said the correct card.

And there it would be, under the tablecloth, halfway down the table. Impossible, simply impossible. No one ever said, "The kid told me to say it!" If the person failed to name the proper card he just moved on to another trick and no one was the wiser. Eventually, he discovered that even if I was not there to collaborate, he could catch the attention of the right suggestible person and flash the bottom card so their eye would be drawn to it. A high percentage of the time, without knowing why, they'd name it correctly. It was one of those human snares that certain shrewd deceivers have a knack for setting.

He was a teetotaler his whole life up until then, but when he entered into his protracted divorce with my mother, he started drinking for the first time. Like Grover Ruwe at the bar with his dummy, my father was now close enough to his audience to take advantage of the offered drink. He found a strategic time to say, "By the way, I drink bourbon and water." The glasses began lining up next to him. Bourbon and water was the only thing he drank because, he said, "It's the only thing I can trust." What was that supposed to mean? How do you *trust* a drink? It was a statement odd enough to present another mystery about him, one that hinted at an answer that was to come only after his ashes were scattered in the Gulf of Mexico.

In our collaborative ruses my father and I developed a repertoire of nods and gestures so subtle as to border on the telepathic. They put us ever deeper into a world of secrets that could only be shared by two people. When he was ready to leave, all he had to do was look my way and I knew it was time to get the LeSabre and pull it around to the front. He got in and I drove him away, never to be seen again. Entertainers seldom had the luxury of sleeping off intoxication—they drove it off. Although my father was fortunate to have me at the wheel, he could have done it without me too.

"Where next, Poppa?"

He gave a long sigh of weariness and pain as he stared into the night. "Just keep going...just keep going."

He'd quickly nod off, but at precisely the right time, many miles later, wake up and say go left or go right, then fall asleep again. A map was always in his head whether he was asleep or awake.

•••

AT A COUNTRY CLUB outside a town long since lost to memory, I met someone from my past. He still had the boyish looks and the long hair carefully combed back, but his face was red and there was no longer a star-point of light in each eye. They were the eyes of a fish, a dead one. He reeked of booze. I couldn't bring myself to show him the *Dorian Gray* in my pocket as if it were an agate, nor could he show me the flat pint in his pocket as if it were a star map. After he and my father changed into their wardrobe in the club locker room with its complimentary colognes in front of the mirror, we waited for the banquet guests to finish their deserts. I was not quite sure what to say to him at this point. He was more forthcoming than I was and told me about his kids in Kansas City, two girls and his youngest, an eight-year-old boy.

"He's fucking every girl in the neighborhood," he said.

"Huh?"

I heard him clearly enough, but I was startled to hear words like that from the Prince of Pantomime, who did "nothing obscene." I assumed it was a sign that he could talk to me as an adult and not have to mind his language on my account. But I did not want to be an adult. I didn't want to hear what his son did. I wanted to be the kid who followed him out to the car under the stars where he packed his record player and harmonicas next to the dinosaur eggs. But it was not going to be that, not now or ever again. Instead, I was left wondering how a boy in the third grade would even be capable of doing what I'd just heard.

The only thing different about Billy's act was that he now used a reel-to-reel tape recorder instead of a record player for *The Barber of Seville*. Everything else was exactly the same: sawing down a tree, the "Old Sow Song," swallowing the harmonica, hair over his face. It was a solid boilerplate of well-worn patter, outdated jokes, and throwaway lines forged and tempered by thousands of audiences, and it still got the intended reaction. Even though he'd become an automaton, there was still something reassuring about the Prince of Pantomime doing what he always did, like some old backstreet business that continued operating after everything around it had been torn down and replaced by something else.

My father gave me the glance as signal to drive around to the front and pick him up, none too sober himself. While I waited, I saw Billy, with a large wet spot in the front of his pants, staggering to his own car with no one to drive for him on the long journey back to Kansas City. To me he was still the genius with dinosaur eggs who knew the names of all the faint stars.

•••

GRANDPA JURAJ SOLD HIS log cabin in Black River Falls and moved to a rooming house in Whiting, Indiana, where he began his immigrant life in 1907 cleaning toxic chemical tanks for Standard Oil. It was here that my uncle, his youngest son, visited him for the first time since he had disappeared decades before.

"I went to this dingy rooming house in a run-down neighbor-hood," he told me after both my parents were dead and I was still living as a transient. "The door to his room was open, but he wasn't there. Maybe he was down the hall in the bathroom. All I re-member was a bare table with a bottle of whisky setting in the mid-dle. When he saw me he said, 'who are you?' and I said 'I'm your son, Bill.' He didn't seem all that thrilled to see me, but we sat down anyway and I told him about my family and kids, and he said a few things that didn't make any sense. I'm not good at small talk, so after a while I left."

Shortly after that, Grandpa Juraj died. On the death certificate my mother's name is given as "informant" and stamped "belated." Cause of death was "atherosclerotic heart disease" and "cirrhosis of liver." She arranged the funeral, which no one attended except her. He left behind nine Warranty Deeds for property, all acquired from women for "one dollar and other good and valuable considerations." The attorney she hired to look into his assets wrote that his real estate dealings "used a different practice than that which most of us have become familiar." The deeds were worthless. His estate, after expenses, amounted to $2,400, leaving approximately $300 for each of the eight children left behind in his Milwaukee mansion. None of them would ever visit his gravestone, upon which is carved "George Arsulich, Father."

My mother proved that the quest for the absent father is not exclusively the province of the son. Nor is it universal, as her siblings proved. But she found him, whereas they did not.

•••

In the summer before my last year in yet another high school (my sixth), I accompanied my father on a military base tour from the Carolinas to New Mexico set up through Dave Brummet, an agent in Atlanta notorious for scheduling thousand-mile "jumps." Traveling separately was the Tommy Martin Orchestra. Shaking a rabbit in the face of a male GI did not get the same reaction as doing it to a woman, but it still had to be done. As on all USO tours there was the requisite "attractive young female" written into the contract, in this case a contortionist a few years older than me and just starting out in show business. She didn't have a car, so she rode with us. Not quite as versatile as the Human Pretzel from Harvester Show days, she did a backbend on a table to pick up a handkerchief with her teeth and drank a glass of water held by both feet while standing on her forearms. She got due respect at Officer's Clubs and most of the NCO Clubs, but at Enlisted Men's Clubs she had to smile through all manner of catcalls at her spread legs and compromising positions. Afterward, she'd be in tears as my father and the musicians tried to console her. She quit after a couple of weeks and took a bus back to Atlanta. She was replaced by a female singer who didn't do much better.

During our long hours on the road and the occasional stay in a hotel where my father I shared the same bed, we came to find each other amusing as well as inscrutable. I laughed at the way he weighed himself on a penny scale while gorging on a bag of Divinity Candy. He got wise to me after the first time I pressed down on the scale from behind with the toe of my shoe. He couldn't understand why I didn't throw away *Paradise Lost* after reading it like he did with his westerns.

"Because I can never be through reading it."

"Then why start in the first place?"

I remember him flipping through the pages at a truck stop to see what it was that I found so interesting.

"You actually understand this stuff?"

"Not all of it. That's why I keep reading it."

A long, very long silence followed.

In hotels I bragged that I could run up the stairs faster than he could take the elevator. When the door opened on the fourth or fifth floor I'd be there, waiting—standing on my hands. That was something he could appreciate.

Sometimes the joking got a little rough, not out of malice, but a combination of careless risk and not knowing when to quit. He did a trick he called "The Wineglass," where he put a silk handkerchief over his flattened palm, then, after a simple steal from his sleeve, lifted the handkerchief to reveal a wineglass filled to the top with water and red food coloring to resemble wine. The colorful liquid shimmering in the spotlight was impressive. To prove it was real liquid in a glass (held in before lifting the handkerchief by a rubber doorknob cover), and with no other way to dispose of it, he drank the "wine." One night I decided to substitute the colored water with

174

gin provided by the band's drummer. After downing the red liquid, his eyes rolled over to me off stage. The musicians and I thought it was hilarious, but I could tell by his expression that he did not. He seemed to have some deeper personal resentment to being tricked into drinking alcohol.

He more than got even with me in El Paso. We went to a café across the border in Juarez, where he said, "Here's your soup," and passed me a bowl of hot sauce. After one spoonful I ran into the bathroom and guzzled water from the faucet, neither of us knowing that tap water in Juarez was not safe to drink. As we proceeded on Brummett's infernal tour across the desert I came down with dysentery. At Laughlin Air Force Base, I got some pills from the dispensary before continuing to Randolph Air Base, then nonstop across Mississippi and Alabama to Ft. Benning and Ft. McPherson in Georgia, then back to New Mexico again. When I finally recovered from the hot sauce prank, I was weak and had lost a lot of weight.

Air conditioning was not common in cars then and the humid heat was unbearable whether the windows were up or down. The panting rabbit suffered as much as we did, the fur on its pink nose soaked with sweat. We carried the poor creature concealed in its black salesman's case into air-conditioned cafés just to keep it alive. We were traveling east again through Mississippi and Alabama and it would have been nice to spend a half hour every now and then at a swimming pool almost every town had, but they were all "closed for repairs" rather than follow the new integration laws. Because our car had Illinois license plates, we were sometimes suspected of being civil rights agitators from the North and followed until we were far enough away to no longer be of concern.

When the military base tour was over we drove immediately from Georgia to Montana for another circuit of grandstand shows booked through the Clarence Smith Agency and consisting of the usual scenery panels (painted with new scenes each year) set up and broken down each night and stored in a truck next to the stage with the orchestra's instruments. As entertainment it was already an anachronism soon to be replaced by top-40 musical acts like Conway Twitty and Bobby Darin. That year my father emceed a lineup featuring Alfredo Landon and his Little People, two midgets and a dwarf who did acrobatics and balanced on poles. Alfredo was normal-sized and worked his little people as if they were trained animals. One of them had a hostile attitude, a basis for our being chums. If a local on the fairgrounds stared at him, he'd go "Boo!" then point and laugh. Also featured was a male singer who did Bobby Darin and Pat Boone songs, and a father and daughter dance team from Hungary. There was a knife-throwing act from Argentina billed as Adolfo and Marta. She did a backbend with a potato on her throat, then he swung a machete and cut it in half without touching her neck. "With your mother-in-law you don't even need the potato…" He made violent chopping motions while trailing off into Spanish, which cracked up Alfredo's hostile little person.

My father was making good money, but all of it went to lawyers and my mother's creditors, so instead of staying in hotels we slept in sleeping bags out in the open. One morning we woke up in a corral next to the grandstand surrounded by grazing pigs. We bought slabs of meat and cans of beans and cooked them over a fire in city parks. A river usually ran through town and that was where we took a bath. Our shared odyssey brought us even closer together and it seemed like it would never end. Afternoons we watched the rodeo that was booked separately on the same circuit. Our favorite event was the most dangerous, the bull riding. There were two rodeo clowns, Frank Curry from New York City and a black man known as "Snowball." Curry wore clown makeup and Snowball stayed as he was. Both were regularly butted over the corrals, pinwheeling through the air like tossed dolls, but they always went back for more. Both were so knocked around and bruised they could hardly walk.

I fell into a drooling lust for the comely and compliant Hungarian girl who danced with her father, both refugees from the Soviet invasion of their country in 1956. As my strength returned from the hot sauce caper, she taught me acrobatic lifting, which we practiced on hard ground with no spotters. After the grandstand show we walked around the fairgrounds arm in arm like a couple of local sweethearts. She and her father slept in a tent they set up behind the stage, and late at night we'd find whatever privacy there was, usually around corrals and grunting livestock. The first Hungarian word I learned was *szúnyog* (mosquito), and both of us had bites where people are not normally bitten. Everyone on the show knew what was going on and at one point my father said to me, "Be careful. I don't trust that girl."

There was that word again, "trust."

Don't trust a drink, don't trust a girl…

•••

THE TOMORROW THAT SEEMED would never come finally did, and the tour ended. The performers went separately to other towns, and other towns after that, and none of us would ever see each other again. My father and I drove straight through from Wyoming to Milwaukee so I could start my sixth high school, the newly opened Brookfield East. I would be in the first graduating class. I showed up late and there was the usual confusion over my not being registered and having no address. I explained the grandstand shows and my parents' divorce. Luckily for me, the new principal was understanding. "I was shifted around as a teenager myself," he said.

For the first month, to fulfill the school's residency requirement, my father put me up in a motel barely within the city limits of Brookfield while he was away on engagements. There was no school bus anywhere near the motel, so I hitchhiked to school, where I enjoyed a certain notoriety because of my past sightings in police cars. I was hoping Craig Tyler and I would be classmates, but while I was out West he got his mother's permission to join the Marines at age seventeen. There were other pariahs at Brookfield East, though, and we found each other soon enough.

In the world of other teenagers, I was as invisible as a dressing room kid, but I wanted to be visible. I copied the Prince of Pantomime's hair style by letting the top grow extremely long and combing it back so no one could tell how long it was until I shook it over my face in a bid for attention, which was minimal. Cleats on boy's shoes were a common nonconformity at the time, the pedestrian version of a loud muffler, so I put them on the heel *and* toe of my shoes and clickety-clacked like Mr. Rhythm down the halls of Brookfield East. As if that weren't enough, I wore a black leather jacket accessorized by white dress gloves left over from an all-boys Catholic military school the court put me in where I lasted all of five weeks. These affectations might not have gotten me as much attention as I was seeking at school, but it did get me noticed by certain older men who picked me up hitchhiking. Sometimes they invited me to look in the glove compartment where they had placed a can of beer and newsstand magazines of sailors and cowboys in jockstraps.

Since floor shows as we knew them had all but disappeared, we no longer met twelve-minute talents in crowded dressing rooms. My father's business became more solitary with one or at most two performers taking up stage time that used to be filled by seven. The hand balancers, tumblers, Simul-talkers, and Human Pretzels of the world, who assumed it would go on forever, disappeared in one mass extinction. All the God-knows-whats who devoted a lifetime perfecting a six- to eighteen-minute routine had to find other work. Television, which they were supposedly "the stars of," exposed and then overexposed what they did until they no longer had commercial value. Less money went around to fewer people. Spies for AGVA didn't skulk around nightclubs and banquet rooms looking for non-union members. Child Protection no longer cared about underage tumblers in strip clubs. Time took care of that for them. My father had no need to rehearse the orchestra because there were no more orchestras. He threw away his sheet music and pulled cards out of the air in silence. We sometimes made visits to a dance studio or furniture store or bathroom tile showroom where an erstwhile Risley act or pogo stick trumpet player had managed to find other employment, sometimes with a dated publicity photo of themselves on the wall like the picture of a deceased loved one. They'd talk about the old days and were sometimes hard to get away from. They would follow us out to the big LeSabre and look longingly, not at the car, but the road dirt on it.

On one of my visits to Chicago, which entailed missing several more days of school, I helped my father drive through the snow to Des Moines where he was booked at an after-dinner banquet. At the front desk he asked for the "theatrical rate," an antiquated price still on the books at some older hotels that used to cater to vaudeville performers. The clerk looked it up and sure enough, there it was, a price at least thirty years out of date. As he signed in, the front door opened and the winter winds blew in another figure from my past. His eyes were bloodshot and his suit looked like he'd slept in it. I smelled alcohol on his breath long before he reached the counter. It was Mr. Rhythm. He recognized my father but not me. I was too callow and self-conscious to know what to say to the man I used to goof around with in the back seat of our car and who'd influenced me all the way down to my footwear. Even though he was black and intoxicated, the desk clerk welcomed him warmly because times had changed, and he was no longer the out of place Negro he used to be. My father helped him get the theatrical rate too, which he hadn't heard of. As he signed in, he made one of his long-standing racial jests about touching the pen, but it fell flat because the clerk didn't care what he touched. As we walked to the elevators, the carpeting silenced my cleats.

Dinner banquets had always been a traditional part of Midwestern life. People who attended them were mostly of my father's generation and many, like him, were veterans of the War. He produced cards, picked pockets, and shook the rabbit in a woman's face, all in a style and tone with which they were familiar. Then Mr. Rhythm finished things off as he always did. Like the Prince of Pantomime, he hadn't changed a word of his routine. He still did the power stomping and wild shouting, sweated profusely, and did the hot chocolate joke. Amusing enough, but I can't say he knocked 'em outta their damn chairs like he used to. The Civil Rights Movement (in which his mentor, Paul Robeson, took a leading part) was at its height, and audiences were no longer unified in the way they perceived African-Americans. The prejudicial assumptions on which "the Scandinavian folk dancer" based his entire existence were now fragmented. This bizarre Other with his camped-up "colored" routine with bobbing head and trilby hat was one more amusement going the way of the freak show. It would not be long before he would disappear altogether in the cold silence of oblivion.

From the inventory of an archival photo merchant, I recently found a black-and-white publicity photo of Teddy Qualls. It was taken some time in the 1950s and had been sitting around someplace a very long time. The photographic quality is not good, nothing like the expensive Maurice Seymour studio shots everyone else had taken. I look at his image for something recognizable, but he is strangely foreign, merely a sign for something he was supposed to be. He sits in a chair in order to bring into closer proximity his face and dancing feet. I'm reminded of the stunt where he sat in a chair and made each of his feet tap differently at the same time. Publicity photos of that period had a dark, noirish quality to them, but in this case there is white everywhere. White background, white hat, white coat, white socks. One arm hangs down to his side with a finger pointing in the direction of his tap shoes as if to divert attention away from his smiling (black) face. I remember in the back seat when I tried to catch that finger in my fist but never could. He always caught mine, but sometimes he let me get away.

Afterward, backstage, I heard the heavy clack of steel taps on the bare floor as he labored over to sit down in a thick smog of booze. He put each betapped patent leather shoe—cracked and shiny on the top, dusty on the bottom—in its own well-worn cloth bag and returned it to a battered case. I was aware of my cleats and tried to keep them quiet, but his ears were tuned to that kind of sound and when he heard a single clack, he looked up at me with sad, red eyes. Neither of us, for our own reasons, was capable of saying anything.

Because I was late in starting classes at Brookfield East, I missed the announcement about class photos, so when the yearbook came out, I was listed as "not shown."

FOURTH ATTRACTION

THE NEW PLACE

WHEN I ENROLLED AT THE University of Wisconsin, Milwaukee, my father thought I was on the way to "making something of myself," but I didn't last there any longer than at other schools. Wandering off the grounds had always been a tendency of mine. It frequently got me into trouble elsewhere, and it was no different at UW-M, where I wandered off campus into profound difficulties for myself, as well as the discovery of difficulties just as profound for my father. In a strange way they were connected, each *because of the war.*

My mother (still moving from couch to couch) wanted me to join a fraternity and associate with students who would be tomorrow's leaders, not tomorrow's magicians. She had a vision of me thriving on campus activities, like photography club or golf league, but as a dressing-room kid, those activities were not for me. I lived in a series of readily available sleeping rooms for transients near downtown on a twenty-dollar a week stipend from my father. When my surroundings became too dreary, I packed my suitcase and found another room.

On weekends, instead of attending university events, I went to Chicago to visit my father. He had signed a management agreement with the Charles Hogan Agency in the 203 North Wabash Building, the theatrical center of America, where agents specialized in booking everything from demolition derbies to lounge harpists. They signed him on not because he pulled cards out of the air, but because he could memorize a current *Look Magazine*, using the mnemonic system I copied and used to pass tests in the classes I skipped. He distributed the pages and as quickly as they were called out, he told what was on them. It made him unique, like the man who could spell any word backward ("Professor Backwards") or Erwin Corey ("World's Foremost Authority"), who could improvise interminable nonsense and make it sound superficially profound. The Hogan Agency booked their entertainers at prestige venues like Mr. Kelly's, the Palmer House, the Copacabana, the Playboy Clubs, exclusive resorts, and all the rooms in Vegas. Although these acts were not famous, they were several levels of status above Billy Papon and Grover Ruwe and all the others who used to stay at our shaky house in the field to save a hotel bill. No one would recognize their names any more than they would recognize my father's, but they were successful enough to live in penthouses overlooking Lake Michigan and drive Lincolns and Cadillacs. They were comics like Sonny Mars, Stu Allen, Mike Caldwell, Lenny Collier, the Goetsche Brothers dance duo, and Johnny Johnstone, the comedy magician who toured with Elvis before anyone had heard of Elvis. They belonged to an exclusive organization called the Three Sheeters, the name referring to top-billed performers of the past who required three sheets for extra-large advertising posters. The Three Sheeters maintained a suite in the Sheraton Hotel downtown with a fully stocked bar so that club members could take a nap or a nip or both whenever they flew in from out of town and had a few hours to kill before appearing at one of the city's top night spots.

Like my mother, my father wanted me to have the best opportunities, so he brought me to the Hogan office to see what real success looked like. My father especially wanted me to meet Mr. Hogan himself, because he was a very, very important person. "He handles only one act," he told me in the elevator. "Bob Hope. During Prohibition, when Hope was a nobody, Hogan booked him in speakeasies. When Hope became famous, he showed his appreciation by accepting an engagement from him every few years that generated enough commission to pay for running the office. Now compare that to Billy Papon. He called me last week at three o'clock in the morning and said he needed ten thousand dollars. I said, 'Billy, I don't have ten thousand dollars.' I didn't even ask what it was for because I knew it had to do with another one of his harebrained business schemes. A few days later I was on the phone with Associated Artists in Des Moines. They said they booked him on a grandstand show somewhere in the South and put him in charge of collecting money from the Fair Board to pay the acts. After closing night, instead of paying the acts, he drove away with the money. They found him somewhere in Texas, sitting in his car along the roadside, out of gas, the money next to him on the seat. He had no idea where he was or how he got there."

We entered the office and found ourselves in the middle of what was called "Happy Hour," when the agency's comics and crooners who happened to be in town milled around the reception area swilling down liquor from bottles and glasses set out on the reception desk. Officially it was supposed to start at four, but the time could be pushed back as early as noon. They were all of my father's Greatest Generation and formed an old-boys club of hardcore stage acts. They had a tough-guy manner to them, like you'd see in old black-and-white movies. Where age quickly pushes hand balancers and contortionists off the stage, it actually enhances the prestige of comics and singers, though their tuxedo façades hid ailments ranging from cardiac dysfunction, liver damage, failed lungs, and other belabored organs, as well as the fog of medication. In my father's case it was arthritic knees. Nor was he the only one in the room losing a large portion of his earnings to lawyers and alimony. Other Happy Hour guzzlers had ex-spouses too, sometimes several, and kids they didn't know the ages of. Summons servers had a way of weaseling into the festivities because they knew it was the easiest place to find their targets. The summons servers knew what they looked like from publicity photos furnished by the ex. Once they found the defendant, they quickly shoved the summons at them and departed under a barrage of derisive zingers.

Each entertainer gave me an overly enthusiastic handshake, some holding it a long time while they remarked on how I resembled my father or joked about how they envied my youth and presumed virility. One power drinker commented on how I'd grown, even though he'd never seen me before.

"Whatcha reading there, Jack Junior?" said one, lifting Elizabeth Bishop's *Questions of Travel* to see the title. "Poetry! I had an uncle used to read poetry books. Carried 'em around in his purse, hey!"

After the handshakes were out of the way, I went back to being invisible, and they went back to gossiping over who'd been on TV recently, who'd been in trouble with the IRS, or who'd been thrown out by the latest spouse.

A grandmotherly secretary who acted as romper room monitor brought us into Mr. Hogan's office. It resembled an Edward Hopper painting, with only a file cabinet and a bare desk with a telephone. Charles Hogan was small in stature and looked like he stepped out of the 1920s with his short, broad tie, and pinstripe trousers pulled up to just below his chest with wide suspenders. He was a quiet man, warm and cordial, holding a cigar stub with one end chewed flat.

"Your father tells me you're in college."

My father spoke up for me. "He's going to make something of himself."

"What's your major?"

"English."

"Is that what you're reading?"

I held up the Bishop volume.

Hogan was not a comedian, so he didn't respond with a joke. Instead, after looking at the title, he studied the chewed end of his cigar in a long moment of reflection and said nothing.

We went to the adjoining office to meet Hogan's partner, Marcus Glaser, who handled all the other comics, tappers, and crooners, as well as my father. It was almost as bare as Hogan's, consisting of a file cabinet and a desk with a telephone and giant ledger where he kept track of all the performers he was booking and how much they owed him in commissions, which was twenty percent off the top, and half of that to Hogan. He was a slow-talking, bald man in his fifties who always sounded like something was stuck in his throat. He wore fine quality, tailor-made shirts and expensive cufflinks, requisite tribute gifts from the performers he represented. The phone rang constantly as calls came in from all over the country. There was such a demand for acts that his sales talk came down to a stock phrase, "Which one of my bums can I sell ya today?" Each booking was concluded in less than a minute.

He said to my father, "So your son's in college, I hear. That's good. At least he's not a pinhead. That's better than that *meshugana* kid of mine. He's living in my house and not doing anything with his life, so one night we have an argument. He disappears for weeks and I'm worried to death, calling the police, calling hospitals, trying to find out where he is. I go home one day and find one of his cigarette butts in the ashtray. He was in the house whole time, sleeping there during the day and going somewhere else when I came home at night. You're on the right track. Stay in school, study business, you'll do fine."

When we rejoined the Happy Hour festivities, one of the comics was in the middle of a story.

"...so he goes in the hospital for heart surgery, but he's got a show coming up at Mr. Kelly's. He checks out early against his doctor's orders and goes on stage and starts doing Sinatra stuff. He's singing 'My Heart Bleeds' and blood starts oozing out the sutures and soaking through his tuxedo shirt. The audience thinks it's some kind of gag, like he's got a pump gimmick under his shirt. When he realizes blood is soaking through, he starts acting like it *is* part of the act. The crowd goes nuts!"

The gagman, helping himself to another generous pour, turned to me. "So, Jack Junior. Won't be long before you to get the ol' draft notice, eh?" He gave my hair a playful tousle and several long strands fell out of place and hung down to my chin like Billy Papon. "You can say goodbye to that funny hairdo. Ha!"

•••

It was mandatory that all male freshmen at the University of Wisconsin, Milwaukee attend Reserved Officers Training Corp (ROTC) classes. There were no assignments, no tests. All we had to do was be present in a large, theater-style lecture hall. To make sure no one skipped out they assigned us seats, and uniformed recruiters with a clipboard took attendance. My father urged me to consider ROTC seriously so that when I inevitably went into the service I would go in as a second lieutenant with what he said would be "easier duty and higher pay."

"Your brother, Jerry, has done very well for himself as an officer in the air force," he told me. "He's now designing rockets that go into outer space. It's all so complicated I can't even begin to understand it. He's about to be promoted to lieutenant colonel. In just a few years he'll be able to retire with a nice pension. As for me, I'll have to keep working on these bad legs for the rest of my life."

The war in Vietnam was never mentioned in ROTC class, even though at the time it was supported by seventy-five percent of the

American public. Strangely, there was little talk of it on campus either, as if it were something distant and not worth thinking about. It soon came to everyone's attention, however, when two undergraduate art students set up an installation in the Student Union titled "Hiroshima, Vietnam, and You." A looping sixteen-millimeter film showed a nuclear explosion on a translucent screen so it could be viewed from both sides. Large crowds gathered to witness this defiance of conventional opinion. After the first day several ROTC cadets in uniform tried to tear it down. The artists and a few of their supporters tried to stop them. A riot ensued, with punching and kicking and overturning tables and hitting each other with chairs. There were injuries. Police had to be called in to break it up. University authorities as well as local TV stations blamed the artists for instigating the riot and the dean of students said the exhibit was "a historically irrelevant way to mischaracterize the Vietnam War."

•••

EVERY SCHOOL I ATTENDED, INCLUDING UW-M, had their baseball, basketball, and football tournaments. It was the focus of school spirit, the stuff of legend. I was no more interested in their sports teams than they were in me. I did, however, have an interest in physical culture. Lifting weights was an end in itself. There were no bleachers of cheering fans. It all came down to a private contest between myself and gravity, which I strove to defeat in a slow, deliberate, and repetitious process.

On my way to and from the YMCA weight room in downtown Milwaukee, I noticed Wisconsin Avenue becoming more and more crowded with sailors from Great Lakes Naval Base. This increased to the point where cops in shiny knee-high boots had to stand at every intersection to prevent mass jaywalking. Shore patrol police vans were everywhere. Many of the sailors stayed in rooms at the Y, where a few went directly to the showers and spent a lot of time there. Others hung out in the weight room, a favorite place for compulsive talkers because they had a captive audience. What they talked about never had anything to do with what I heard in ROTC class. Instead, they regaled us with long and detailed stories about a place called Saigon, where naked teenage girls performed unimaginable stunts with marbles, goldfish, and cigars, and were available afterward for private entertainment. And there was a more ominous topic.

After a set of bench presses, one well-scrubbed young man who looked as fresh as any ROTC cadet, but with an incongruously rough manner that seemed recently acquired, said, "Those counterinsurgency guys are psychos. They come back after a week in the jungle with fly-covered strings of human ears. That's how they keep track of the enemy body count. Some of those ears are pretty small too. Our lieutenant didn't care what they did as long as they brought back ears. Over there, every fucking man, woman, and child is the enemy. The gooks even rig up babies with booby traps. Or they dig holes covered with brush and put sticks at the bottom sharpened to a point and smeared with shit. Out in the jungle, just a scratch can get infected, but one of those shit sticks piercing halfway up your leg could kill you. One guy stepped on one and got gangrene. The VC had already killed our medic and no one knew what to do. We didn't have any morphine because some guys used it all to get high, so they stuffed a bunch of dirty socks down the guy's throat to shut him up, then shot his leg off below the knee just to save his fucking life. At least he got a medical discharge and went home."

After the riots in the student union I saw a sheet on a bulletin board advertising what was called a "teach-in" about US involvement in Southeast Asia. Out of curiosity, I attended. It was a disorganized session that was supposed to be about the history of foreign intervention but was actually a forum on ways to dodge the draft. One of the facilitators was a former classmate from Brookfield East, another loner I hadn't seen for a while. Upon graduation he did not enroll in college and was promptly drafted and sent to Vietnam.

"They made me hide in a swamp," he said, "with muck up to my nose. I told my NCO I couldn't swim but he made me stay there for hours with orders to shoot anyone who passed by—anyone, no exceptions. Old women, kids, they were all the enemy. I just stayed high on marijuana all the time and let everyone go by. When they didn't find any bodies on the road, they took me out of the swamp and sent me out on patrols. A guy behind me stepped on a land mine and got blown up into a tree. I just missed stepping on the same land mine myself. We took incoming fire from all directions while he hung there in the tree with blood dripping down. We passed dead women and kids snipered by the guy who replaced me in the swamp. I couldn't take it anymore, so I shot off my big toe and said it was an accident. Funny how many other guys had the same accident. Anyway, I got a medical discharge. Also, free tuition under the GI Bill."

Someone mentioned that going to the induction center in a dress could result in being judged mentally unfit for duty. Another student said you could get the coveted 4-F classification if you grew a Hitler mustache and showed up at your physical wearing a swastika, but my friend added, "That's more likely to get you accepted than rejected." There was mention of "punitive reclassification," where you could lose your student deferment if undercover agents found out you were at a teach-in like this one.

For all the summers I spent at county fairs, I should have been as enthused by patriotism as I was by hogs and horses. Fairgrounds were, and still are, the natural habitat of flags. They cluster at the ticket gates. They rise from the tops of exhibit buildings and sprout from the bandstand next to the stage. Fair managers often insisted the grandstand show begin with the National Anthem and flag-bearing squads of American Legionnaires marching down the track. Flags were as traditional as the grandstand show itself. Performers were invited to join town parades in full wardrobe, driving their cars with the road dirt washed off especially for the occasion. A juggler would march along while juggling Indian clubs and sequined acrobats proceeded with intermittent cartwheels. Our car slowly moved in a gap between drum-beating marchers carrying American flags, state flags, banners, and scrims that united the crowd in collective patriotic exuberance. From the driver's seat my father, in his frock coat and bow tie, projected his stage smile and my mother beamed hers from the passenger side. From the back seat I leaned out and waved at the parade watchers who waved back.

•••

WHEN HE NEEDED ZINC stearate for his cards, or new silk scarves of specific size and color for the rabbit trick, my father went to Jay Marshall's Magic, Inc., the illusion supply store on Lincoln Avenue in Chicago. Here, the atmosphere was completely different than the Hogan Agency. The lights were dim, and the place felt like a museum. On shelves behind the counter were colorful boxes with mystical symbols emblazoned on the side, chrome devices of cryptic function, curious cylinders, and bouquets of feathers arranged like decoration on an altar. To add just the right note of overall uncanniness, there was a small, mass-produced ventriloquist dummy leaning askew on a high shelf. For every enticing piece of apparatus visible on the shelves and in the cabinets, there were a hundred others in the back room.

As a variation on the prop-touching taboo, no one was permitted to handle anything until after they bought it. A customer could look from a distance, ask questions, and maybe Jay or his wife Frances or one of the clerks would demonstrate it *once*. It was understood that at Magic, Inc., or any such store like it, a person is never buying a trick, they are buying a secret. The store attracted hobbyists so dedicated to this world of illusion that they practically lived there.

They formed cliques based on the number of secrets they knew, and if you were properly connected in the right circles (which was not easy and took a long time) you could obtain outrageously expensive illusions built by prestigious craftsmen. Some of the magicians were well-known within the trade, like Jack Kodell or Jay Marshall himself, both having been on *The Ed Sullivan Show*, but unknown to the general public.

Magic apparatus did not inspire my father and he had no interest in talking about it. Magic, Inc. was merely a place to pick up supplies he couldn't get anywhere else. He barely concealed his disdain for the hobbyists and collectors, who were vastly more knowledgeable on the topic than he was. To him, success was not a matter of how many secrets you knew or how many tricks you did but how much money you made. To be exclusively signed with the Hogan Agency and appear at Playboy Clubs or "the Cope" (Copacabana) meant one had to offer more than a bunch of tricks off a shelf. There had to be one-liners, manipulated stooges, stolen watches, a memorized magazine, and a woman shocked by a rabbit thrust in her face—all after fifty or sixty hours without sleep. And the biggest trick of all was hanging onto the money once you made it.

My own knowledge of the conjuring arts went as far as how to put away my father's props, which I'd been doing since the dawn of my conscious life. I didn't care about stuff on the shelves either. I had no more in common with the magicians at Magic, Inc. than I did with the comics and crooners at the Hogan agency. To both groups I was invisible, as I was everywhere else. Except to my parents.

And one other person about to emerge from my past. Had I not internalized my father's cautionary allegories from behind the wheel, I might have succumbed more than I did to the influence of that person who came, like me, from a background not preparatory for everyday life. One afternoon at the Y, when I brought my homework to that mirrored sanctuary of focused concentration, there was a note waiting for me at the desk. It read, "Meet me in lobby at 5—Craig Tyler."

He must have remembered when I skipped school to hitchhike to the Y and took a chance that I might still be found there. Otherwise, like my father, I'd be untraceable. At five o'clock he was not in the lobby. At five-thirty, he was still not there. I was ready to leave when a heavyset figure with a GI haircut and sunburned face walked in carrying a government issue duffle bag with "US Marines" on the side. It was a reunion of the dugout kid and the dressing room kid.

"Vietnam" was the first word he said followed by "Bad Conduct Discharge."

The reason he was in Milwaukee was because he didn't have enough money for a train ticket all the way to Boston, where his mother and sisters had moved. I welcomed him to sleep on the floor of my room and share my ration of rutabaga (the cheapest food available, at six cents a pound) and bulgur (free from the county). He readily accepted.

"At least there's no snakes," he said.

With nothing to constrain us, we made up for lost time. I told him about the rodeo clowns, my Hungarian girlfriend, the machete-wielding knife thrower, the Prince of Pantomime, and Happy Hour comics at the Hogan Agency. He told me about "drilling gooks," going AWOL, robbing taxi drivers in San Diego, punching his NCO, and landing in the brig. I took him into all the places I went when I wandered off campus: the Art Museum, the Zoo, the Renaissance Bookstore, and poetry readings at a bohemian coffeehouse called the Avant Garde. For his part he brought me into bars where he struck up aggressive conversations with sailors and taunted the military police parked on Wisconsin Avenue. Sometimes there was a scuffle.

"In the marines you learn to travel light," he said. "Anything you need along the way you steal it. Food, ammo, even a jeep." To prove it he snuck through any door that was unlocked, not knowing where it would lead. I went with him, going even farther afield from the university campus. If we were caught some place we weren't supposed to be, he'd show a perverse charm and say something like, "We were looking for a bus stop" or "I lost my cat." If they challenged him, he said with disarming aplomb, "I just came from Vietnam where I—" then describe some chilling atrocity followed by, "so my life means nothing to me." It was the talk of the battle-hardened. They backed away and we calmly retreated. But sometimes he encountered a veteran of the same or some other war who recognized the threatening talk for what it was. If it happened to be a marine, they'd exchange details of their units and deployments and end up shaking hands and parting with *"semper fi."*

The term was not used yet, but Craig must have had what is now called post-traumatic stress. *Because of the war.* My room started to fill with staplers, toothpick dispensers, wastebaskets, and typewriters, as well as a swivel chair and an oxygen tank I talked him out of using to blow up a candy store. He forced confrontations with people in cafés because they made noise when they ate and "gave away their position." I looked on as he kicked over furniture in bars and cleared countertops in one sweep because people were acting like "Charlie" (the Vietcong enemy). The bullied fat kid now bullied the world. He spent the night in jail a couple of times for disturbing the peace, but when he flashed his old military ID and cited his service in Vietnam, his cases were "continued" and he was sent on his way with a pat on the back. The BCD never came up.

Meanwhile, at newsstands, headlines read "War Escalates," "Draft Calls Rise," "Protests Increase." As long as I stayed enrolled at the University, my student deferment kept me safe. The one class I could not skip was ROTC, where attendance was mandatory. So I continued to sit through lectures on leadership, military culture, and surface warfare (but no mention of Vietnam). While the recruiters spoke, my head was a riot of repetition: *shot off his leg... hung in a tree...human ears...*

After the last session, when the officer in charge made a final pitch to sign up, I was among the first to rush out.

•••

MEANWHILE, CRAIG WOULD VANISH for a day or two then suddenly reappear with new clothes and enough cash to continue buying drinks and literally kicking his way around Milwaukee bars. Since he was the only friend I had, I went along. In my long history of wandering off the school grounds, I was always able to keep my grades up, but wandering off campus took me so far away from my studies that even with my memory systems, I fell behind. When Craig scraped together enough money to buy a bus ticket to Boston, I dropped out of college and went there with him—not a good idea for any draft-age male concerned about his student deferment.

His mother and two sisters now lived in a small apartment under conditions more decrepit than before. Her drinking had gotten worse, and her hugs and kisses and glass after glass of sherry and telling me how much she loved me became oppressive. She still harangued Craig as a "no good bahstid," and whenever his aunt, a nurse, came by for a visit, she made it known that I was the source of all the dysfunction. They all began to believe it, including myself.

Craig managed to lie his way into an unusually well-paying job at a chemical company, using his status as a Vietnam vet (not mentioning the BCD), and got his own apartment where I was not invited to stay because, he said, he had a girlfriend. I last saw him at a trolley stop in Newton, where he was in a sharp new suit and on the way to work. Staying alone in his mother's apartment was out of the question, so I rented a four-dollar-a-week room on Chandler Street in the skid row section of the Back Bay and started going to Boston University, not as a student, but as a scullion, cleaning ovens in the cafeteria kitchen.

Mrs. Ferris, my landlady, must have wondered who I was among her bottom-feeding tenants to receive so many letters on stationery from places like the Hotel Georgia in Vancouver, Chalfonte-Haddon Hall in Atlantic City, and the Twenty-Four Carat Club in Detroit. A separate stream of mail with different return addresses came from Milwaukee, in which my mother admonished me for not telling her the whole story of why I suddenly dropped out of college. With her usual abrupt shifts, she wrote about the fencing classes she started at the Jewish Community Center and dinner at the Black Kettle in Brown Deer with the new people she moved in with. There was a man she was seeing from India named Mohanarangan whom she'd met in a button shop. Unknown to me, forces were closing in on my invisibility, which I would have to evade by calling upon a lifetime of experience in the art of deception.

Pyle's Prestidigitation

Jack Pyle, master of ceremonies for the Midland Empire State Fair's night show, entertains people with card tricks—but it takes less than half an eye (the other eye and a half being on his hands) to tell that the person who gets every bit as much kick out of his show as anyone in the audience is Pyle himself. (See story—Page 6)—Gazette photo by Norm Hill.

In one of my weekly collect calls to my father he told me about the stranger who came into Happy Hour. "He reminded me of your brother, Jerry," he said. "The comics thought he was a summons server and heaped insults on the poor guy. *Are your shoes the natural color or did you step in something?* Tasteless stuff like that. But he was a good sport about it and asked if he could talk to me in private. We went out in the hall and he identified himself as from the Selective Service and said that the notices they sent you had been returned by the Post Office. He wanted to make sure you knew that you were called up to take your physical in Milwaukee. He asked me how to reach you, and I said all I knew was that you were in the process of moving somewhere out east. I didn't tell them you were in Boston. He said the FBI was already preparing a warrant for your arrest. So I said, look, I think I can solve this. I told him the next time you called I'd tell you to contact the Selective Service in your new location and arrange to take your physical there. It turns out he's an amateur magician and knows a few people at Magic, Inc. He went out of his way to tell me he would try to hold off the authorities for a while and give you a chance to arrange things. There you are."

He did not mention the word "Vietnam," and neither did I.

•••

THE THOUGHT KEPT REPEATING, *warrant for your arrest, warrant for your arrest*... In discarded issues of the *Boston Globe* (since I could not afford to buy one) I read that anti-war protests were gaining momentum and joining forces with the civil rights movement. The House on Un-American Activities Committee (HUAC) was aggressively investigating both movements for Communist infiltration. I went to the Boston Public Library and researched what thus far I had put in denial. There was something called the Smith Statute, part of the Alien Registration Act of 1940, that made it a crime to advocate overthrow of the federal government. Throughout the 1950s, after the Rosenberg trial and the fall of China to the Communists, government informants used the Smith Statute as a pretext to infiltrate a wide variety of organizations, bringing evidence, real or fabricated, against anyone thought to be a Communist or connected with one, or who simply disagreed with government policies. It was used as legal justification to open mail sent to or from any organizations deemed subversive.

As a peripatetic dressing room kid familiar with all the illusions of the stage, I saw people in two categories: those who set traps and those who fell for them. Fortune-tellers could make people think their futures could be read in their palms. A skilled hand balancer could put on a rigged glove and make it look like he was standing on one finger. A dummy without a mouth could look like it's talking. Governments too have their ruses, as Daniel Ellsberg would prove with the Pentagon Papers. Like any magician, I knew that a common assumption could be turned against itself. I pulled my shoulders back, held my head high, and approached the desk at the Boston Public Library. "I am looking for the address of the Communist Party."

The young woman librarian was dumbstruck. She went to confer with a male associate who fixed his gaze upon me as he slowly approached. "Is this the American Communist Party?" he asked in a voice a little too loud for a library, causing several people to look up from their reading. "Or some foreign communist party? There's more than one, you know."

"American. It's for a school assignment." He went away and returned with a piece of paper he dropped on the counter like it was something he didn't want to touch. I walked away with the New York address of Gus Hall, Chairman of the most taboo organization in America. I could almost feel the heat on my fingers.

Writing to him was like trying to write a thank you note to Grandpa Juraj. I had no idea what to say. I neither studied nor cared about communist ideology. I knew it only as a dark and forbidding topic in the public mind, but I brought myself to compose something like this:

Dear Mr. Hall,

I am interested in becoming a Communist. I have always admired Communism and want to devote myself to the cause of overthrowing the US government. I would like to participate in Communist activities and would be willing to meet someone from the Party to discuss things further, perhaps in the Boston area.

Awaiting your reply,

Etc.

I should at least have read *The Communist Manifesto* and parroted a few phrases about "subjugation of the labor of others," but I didn't have time for that. I was focused on just one thing: having my name seen and recorded as soon as possible under the Smith Statute. My plan was to go in for my physical and let the dastardly information come out on its own.

A week later Mrs. Ferris slipped an envelope under my door with only a street and number for a return address. I ripped it open. There was no personal reply from Gus Hall and no acceptance of my request to meet and discuss communist subversion. All it contained was an order blank for a subscription to *The Daily Worker*. What I did not notice at first was that the letter had already been opened and resealed. On the back, handwritten in small script and covered with a piece of tape, were the words "Smith Act."

I wrote more letters to Gus Hall that were undoubtedly masterpieces of muddle, offering my services as infiltrator, mole, secret agent. If he read them at all, he had to have dismissed me as a common crackpot. It must have been clear I had no idea what the Communist Party actually did aside from how it was characterized in red-scare TV programs and the McCarthy hearings that preempted the *Howdy Doody Show*. If I'd have taken the time to look into it, I would have found that activities of the CPUSA were mostly in the area of labor organizing during the Depression. I didn't know that when we moved to Milwaukee there was a three-term socialist mayor still in office. By then the Communist Party had pretty much gone the way of the floor show, although it was becoming active again in the anti-war movement.

I received from Party Headquarters another notice (with "Smith Act" written on the back) that an anti-war demonstration was planned in downtown Boston. This was early in the protest movement so there were only about a dozen picketers marching in a circle surrounded by an equal number of photographers and a hundred or so jeering spectators. A few of the photographers displayed press credentials and the rest I assumed were undercover agents. Some of the protesters wore sunglasses, scarves, and hats pulled down over their faces to obscure their identity. I made sure my face was fully visible and looked directly at the cameras.

Following that was a lecture at Boston University by Herbert Aptheker, theoretician of the Communist Party USA. He had just made a much-publicized trip to Hanoi with history professor Staughton Lynd of Yale and Tom Hayden, associated with the vilified Students for a Democratic Society. There was an overflow crowd, maybe a thousand or more people, to see this notorious Communist. Uniformed police were in abundance and many photographers took an absurd number of photos, mostly, it seemed, for the purpose of intimidation. I made every effort to get in their frames. Aptheker was also scheduled the next day to speak in Roxbury before about twenty Depression-era Communists. There were no photographers at this meeting, at least none that I could detect. All I saw was a man who sat with his finger in his ear, whispering into his fist as if it were a telephone receiver. I introduced myself to Aptheker but did not have a single intelligent or even cogent thing to say, and he was not interested in talking to me. But at least I was hopefully seen, and maybe clandestinely photographed, in the presence of a known Communist agitator. The war continued to escalate.

•••

FINALLY, IT WAS SHOW time, and I was on. I entered the Military Entrance Processing Station under a banner that read "Freedom's Front Door." As my father always said, "When you walk out there, you walk out there alone." I was among a hundred draftees ordered to strip down to our underwear. We spread our toes, spread our buttocks, opened our mouths, had our ears and nostrils probed and our knees tapped with a rubber hammer. It was done carelessly at top speed because another group was scheduled behind us, then one after that, and so forth for the rest of the day and for weeks and months to come. According to Selective Service records, almost 400,000 young men were called for the draft that year. Anything less than a five-pound tumor on the face was hardly worth noting.

For the vision test a medic said, "Read line five." I barely focused my eyes on the first number when he said, "Now line six." After the first couple of letters he shouted, "Next!" At the hearing exam there were two medics. One held a tuning fork to my ear and asked if I could hear it. Before I could slur out an answer, he clamped a set of earphones on my head and told me to say in which ear I heard certain tones, but before I could say anything he pulled off the earphones and shouted, "Next!"

They could weed out the deaf ones later.

Mental evaluation came last. This was where I had to pull my own cards out of my own air. The worse I looked the better. I was supposed to answer certain written statements by checking a box that read "Completely True" or "Completely Untrue." For the statement "People are out to get me," I checked "Completely True."

For "I feel worthless" I also checked "Completely True." When it came to "I am addicted to drugs" I checked that one "Completely True," as I did to the statements "I hear voices," "I want to harm myself," and "I am fascinated by fire." When it came to the statement "I am homosexual" it was only yes or no and for this I checked the "Yes" box. Then, "Have you ever been a member of the Communist Party or any other organization advocating the overthrow of the United States government?" Subversives can't be truth-tellers, can they? With exquisite misdirection I answered "No" and relied on the Smith Act to catch up with me later.

Throughout the entire process, "Vietnam" was not said once.

•••

To KEEP PACE WITH the repetitions in my head—*people are out to get me, people are out to get me*—I vigorously scrubbed ovens in the BU cafeteria until caustic soda ate the skin off my fingertips. I did such a good job that I was promoted to the night shift, operating a floor polisher. I did an exemplary job with that too, guiding the rotating buffer back and forth, back and forth... *People are out to get me...*

My father was pleased to hear that I took his advice and went in for my physical, but I didn't tell him about my trick with the Smith Act. We each had our private matters to attend and no further questions were needed. While I waited for the dreaded results, he passed on a letter that was sent to him from Associated Artists in Des Moines.

> He hadn't drank for two years. His brain was full of malignant tumors and the doctors said they couldn't even try to guess how many other tumors had developed throughout his whole body. For a while he couldn't swallow or talk but after the chemo-therapy treatments that came back. Of course he lost all of his hair. Betty said that the last weeks his motor control was affected and he fell a lot.

She said Billy didn't want to die but he faced it and was well prepared. He even made his own funeral arrangements. We regret that we were fooled and didn't respond to his call for help when he called us from Texas where he ran away with the money. Thank goodness, we did write him a long letter. Betty said he carried it with him from the time he received it. Billy looked wonderful at his funeral. He had on his show suit and Shrine fez, which covered his baldness.

I twirled a strand of my hair and extended it out the better part of a foot, my memorial to the Prince of Pantomime. I knew everyone I grew up with in terms of reconciling their presence with their absence. One always entailed the other. Billy Papon, like my father, existed largely in the realm of absence, so his death barely changed much. He lived as he always had, as the lone faint star I see in the southern sky when I drive the same roads as he did, a star with a name as unknown as his—Fomalhaut.

The next letter Mrs. Ferris slipped under my door was clearly from the Selective Service. I was tempted to leave it unopened and take up life as a fugitive again, but I came up with the courage to see what was inside. As I expected, it was my new draft card, which I was required by law to carry at all times. Local Board 76 of the Selective Service System in Waukesha, Wisconsin, where my exam results were sent, had rendered their judgment. Every card had a hyphenated number and letter that meant either life or death. If it were a one and an A, then I'd have to consider running away to Canada or shooting off a toe, or resign myself to being the expendable one at the front of a patrol. Technically, burning my draft card could get me five years in prison, but that didn't stop me from striking a match and burning mine on the spot, coward that I was, since a 4-F classification (physically, mentally, and morally unfit) meant I couldn't be drafted anyway.

I told my father the reason I was rejected for military service was because of a back injury from lifting weights at the Y, something I never mentioned before. He didn't bring up the subject again. My mother was more probing, but not by much, dismissing the back injury as a lie and making some vague reference to "honor." She never brought it up again either.

When I left Boston, I had no place to return, no trailer in a nameless town, no shaking house in a field, no dream home in the suburbs. Both my parents were still moving from place to place, and so was I. On some level I was looking for a dressing room where I could go and be invisible again, but I had to settle for being a transient in various cities.

After my performance for the Selective Service, I endeavored to weave myself into what Henry James called "the embroidery of life's canvas." The best I could do was enhance the light at the end of my personal tunnel by replacing the overhead bulb in rented rooms with the highest wattage I could find, turning dreary hovels into a kind of stage set where every crack and flaw, every speck and stain showed in brilliant clarity with me as the center. I even kept the light on at night so in the morning I woke up to a blazing geography of crumbling ceiling and stained wallpaper, the equivalent of a comforting wasteland around a trailer park.

FLYING HIGH AND LOW

W HEN I ARRIVED IN SAN Francisco, instead of clapboard houses and buildings of ochre brick platted beneath cumulus skies, I found steep hills laced with dwellings of pastel pink and blue under a sky devoid of a single cloud. Painted lady mansions were nestled together with no space between them on boulevards lined with palm trees, while gulls circled and squawked overhead in air that smelled of the sea.

I stood at the intersection of a place I'd read about called Haight and Ashbury, a marvelous confluence of Babylon and Carnival. To a background of Hendrix and Jefferson Airplane coming from record stores and poster shops, happy, draft-age peddlers with beards down to their chest strode by muttering "grass-acid-mushrooms," or "hash-Osleys-Michoacan" as if it were all one word. Everyone presumed a mutual connection on some exalted level. Lit joints circulated among friend and stranger alike, and it was considered impolite to refuse. Hello and goodbye were obsolete formalities. After a couple of blocks, I was flying high on the milk of a new paradise. This was worth crossing the boundaries for. Stoned hippies approached me and spoke in Jabberwocky as a kind of prankish tease then dissolved back into the crowd. I'd heard this same sort of non-speak from bally-talkers and operators of rigged games in carnivals as a way to confound local wiseacres who thought they could outwit them. A springy, hirsute gleeman in an Abe Lincoln top hat pointed at me and said, "Hey, look! J. Edgar Hoover!" referring to the suit I was wearing, one of my father's old Kuppleman jobs. I was supposed to have it altered so I could impress important people, but instead I spent the money on books. For the moment it was all I had to wear, and it hung oddly on my body, what with its false pockets and still having been tailored for two bowed legs. By wearing my father's suit, I felt that in some way I had his powers—not of magic, but of fortitude and endurance.

In thick oceanside fog in front of the Fun House at Playland, I tried to insinuate myself into groups of Flower Children under Laffing Sal, the mechanical robot. We were strangers in the same strange land. Even though I didn't have a beard or (visibly) long hair, my ill-fitting suit and willingness to inhale their esprit made me unconventional enough to be included. At least at first. "Magician's son" was an acceptable enough credit, but they expected me to be more, say more, do more. Fit some better image, be more mystical. Pull something out of the air. Disappear. All I could come up with was a little palmistry, which made for some "far outs," but the "shut-eyes" (carnie slang for true believers) among them regarded me as not sufficiently in fashion, so I was excluded.

I gave plasma and worked temp jobs unloading ships on the Embarcadero to make enough to put me up in the Stanley Hotel on California Street, at the foot of Nob Hill. The Stanley was like a small town, with Chris, the motherly manager, presiding over a divergent assemblage of hippies, office workers, students, and retirees, as well as a man in a turban, a trolley driver, and the occupant of the room next to me who had an unusually red face and played his radio too loud. The halls were redolent of incense and cannabis. It was a better place to live than cheaper rooms in the vice-ridden Tenderloin, where I stayed at first, but it was filling up with heroin addicts returning from Vietnam. They carried weapons and lived a desperate life of violence to which they were well adjusted after their tour of duty fighting in the jungles. By comparison the Stanley was a nirvana of comfort. Chris delivered the mail every day by slipping it under the doors. She told me I got more letters than anyone in the hotel. They were all from my parents.

In long, chatty effusions written in fountain pen on dainty letter-writing stationery, my mother chided me for everything I needed chiding for.

> And what do you mean by being in the 'real estate subletting business?' What in the world is that? I've heard enough of your baloney to know when you're lying to me. By the way, do you know you've never sent me a picture taken with that Instamatic I gave you? How's about getting it out and using it? You're in a picturesque city and I'm sure you've met some interesting people. I expect some pictures soon.

She was right about the "baloney." If I let a pothead crash on my floor in exchange for a joint, I considered that "subletting."

My father's letters were written on stationery from hotels and resorts around the country or sent in envelopes he poached from the Hogan Agency, crossing out the agency name and rubber stamping his own over it. He began to mention a mysterious woman named "Jane," an undertaker's widow he met in a park near his latest apartment on Marine Drive. She told him she had a heart problem and was not expected to live more than a few months, though actually she flourished another twenty years and outlived him.

If at one time the trailer was a kind of envelope in which we lived, now the envelope was a kind of trailer. Even though we circulated in different cities, we were just as close by way of letters. Chris slipped one from my father under the door that mentioned someone else from the realm of the absent.

I am enclosing a letter I just got from Jerry. I think he is having some trouble adjusting to the kind of life that he is involved in. I can understand. I was there once myself. I had a wife, but not two kids, and like the rest of our clan, he is very fond of his family. If you can manage it, why don't you drop him a line. One of these days he is going to be the only close relative that you will have—if he makes it back alright. Reading between the lines in his letter, I don't think he is too sure that he will.

He omitted the word that was in the news every day. Enclosed were several pages in a handwriting I recognized from occasional glimpses in trash bags of the past, perfectly formed lines on paper blank as a cloudless sky, straight and spaced as planes in formation. His address was also San Francisco, but instead of a street it was a series of numbers and acronyms to a mail drop in Quang Nam Province, Vietnam. I thought he was still in Florida working on intercontinental missiles.

It was dated, in military style, 18 March, 1970.

Dear Dad,

I was happy to get your letter and find you are back working again. I hope that you don't push too hard and make yourself ill again.

I'm slowly settling into the routine of things here. I don't think I will ever become adjusted to them. This is the first time I've been in an operations outfit for years and I find I'm the second oldest man in it. It seems funny to be looked on as the old man of the outfit. I'm the operations officer and I have the responsibility of running the flying mission.

I fly the same missions as my pilots and I know what it is like to be out there. I feel my years and my responsibility to my family and to the families of every pilot who flies for me. It is the first time I have ever really felt the weight of command. It is an awesome experience.

I need some water bottles to fly with. Some of the fellows have managed to acquire what looks like a plastic hip flask from the prohibition era. Since they are flat the flask can be carried in the calf pocket of a flying suit and being plastic they won't break if you have to bail out. Water is the most important thing to a pilot caught on the ground. Anyway I'd like for you to see if you can find some. I'll need about four of the pint size if you can find them. If you can't find a pint a half pint will do. They just can't be gotten over here.

I went over to personnel section yesterday and made sure that they had my career statement covered since I'll be put into the pool for reassignment next month.

I noticed he ended his letter, "Your son, Jerry," and not "Love, Jerry." I always ended mine, "Love, Jackie," still using my childhood nickname, and his always ended, "Much love, your Dad."

What was he doing in Vietnam, of all places, where I should have gone? He had just been promoted from second lieutenant to major. Although he was trained to fly the F-100, propelling 28,000 pounds of gleaming titanium at 800 miles an hour through the stratosphere and could ascend four miles straight up in one minute with Sidewinder missiles and up to four types of thermonuclear bombs, he was now flying what I later learned was a propeller-driven OV-2 Cessna reconnaissance plane with no armor and no offensive weapons, slower than frontline aircraft in WWI. His orders were to look for Vietcong activity and mark their location with flares so ground patrols could move in and kill them. He flew low enough over the jungle canopy to catch leaves in the landing gear. The fuselage was riddled with bullet holes. What happened to that "easier duty" my father had talked about?

After I torched my draft card in Boston, I thought I was done with Vietnam, but now it claimed all of my attention again. *If you have to bail out…if you have to bail out…* From my exalted sanctuary in the Stanley, I tried to write Jerry as my father had asked, but all I could think of were the huge anti-war demonstrations that were growing increasingly violent. National Guardsmen at Kent State University had just killed four students, some of them bystanders, setting off more massive protests, including one in Washington, DC, where the Sixth Marines went on alert for possible deployment against them. Whatever I wrote rang false. *Dear Jerry, We have a mailing address in the same city… Dear Jerry, They decided not to draft me… Dear Jerry, The azaleas in Golden Gate Park are beautiful… Dear Jerry, Hope your plane doesn't get shot down… Dear Jerry… Dear Jerry… Dear Jerry.*

The letter never got written.

A day or two passed and I was still thinking of something to say. I went to the McClaren Rhododendron Dell in Golden Gate Park to find the words there, but all that came to me was the cool sensation of petals against the palm of my hand. Back at the hotel Chris had slipped a note under my door. "I have a very important telegram for you at my place. Was delivered at 2:05 p.m. and I had to sign for it. Chris." I picked up the telegram and opened it in my room.

JERRY WAS SHOT DOWN IN VIETNAM THIS MORNING NOBODY FOUND IN OR AROUND THE PLANE NO FURTHER WORD AT THIS TIME.

I assumed he had bailed out and made his way to safety with a hip flask of water in the calf pocket of his flying suit. Death only happened to other people. It couldn't happen to him. It gave me another couple of days to think of something to say. *Dear Jerry, Sounds like you had quite the encounter...* Two days later Chris had another telegram for me.

HE WAS EITHER SHOT IN THE PLANE OR OUT-SIDE THE PLANE.

The Air Force offered no further information. No details of the crash or where in Vietnam it happened. For the rest of my father's life he would never know the full story of how Jerry died any more than he would know the full story of how I survived. I faced the same guilt as when the Mongolian aerialist fell to her death after I broke the taboo of talking with her daughter in the bandshell.

My father sank into such utter gloom that it was difficult to be in his presence. Somehow his new partner, Jane, was able to do it, maybe from her previous married life with a mortician, living among the aggrieved. Instead of forcing himself to stay awake, as he'd done for much of his life, now he said he could barely sleep at all, and when he did, he had nightmares of Jerry running for his life through a jungle. My father was not welcome at Happy Hour because he brought no happiness to the hour, so the Agency sent him all over the country for less and less money just to keep him away. With each step he forced himself to gather strength for the next.

If I flew into Chicago for a visit and escorted him to a few performances, I could tell by people's reaction they knew something was wrong. They recognized the 1940s style, which was what they wanted, but he performed like a mis-wired robot. He remembered the magazine pages in his memory stunt but repeated jokes he'd already said. If he quit the stage he would no longer be "busy," and therefore cease to exist. If he kept going, others had to face the problem of what to do with a Master of Deception who failed to cover his unfathomable pain with the shabby remains of a manufactured persona.

By this time his thick, wavy hair was white, but his smile, still framed by a mustache (also white), was radiant as ever in the spotlight. Because of the striking image he more or less maintained, the Hogan Agency booked him as a professional emcee at large corporate events. All that mattered was his apparent gravitas. He was no longer the Master of Deception but the deception itself. Appearing as an elder figure of great eminence, he recited scripts provided by the client that made it seem like he was an expert in the field. His elocution was that of an educated man because it was something he carefully cultivated, but privately said, "I'm strictly a lowbrow." No one knew that his eyesight was so bad he couldn't distinguish male from female without his glasses, nor that his arthritic legs could barely carry him to the podium. On his way in from the car he sometimes sat on the curb until he regained the ability to continue. When it was time to appear, he forced himself into a graceful stride with an act of will comparable to moving a house with a team of mules. He rejected the use of a cane, and when the first handicapped parking spaces were introduced, he refused the special permit because he thought someone might see it and judge him as something less than what he was trying to be. In desperation he arranged to have his bowed legs surgically straightened, but the procedure was so painful for one leg that he did not have it done to the other. It did not make walking any easier, and all his trousers had to be altered on one side by whomever had taken the place of Mr. Kuppleman.

When I drove him to his performances, there were no longer cryptic stories about the dangers that await those who don't see what's ahead. He simply sat in silence. His burden became my burden. After that fateful telegram, a spotlight turned on me as the only surviving son, one who felt guilty for surviving.

He's going to make something of himself…

In truth, I had no immediate prospects aside from giving plasma twice a week at a blood bank in the Mission District and spending the rest of my time reading and taking buses and trolleys to the end of the line and continuing on foot to wherever it would lead until the fog and darkness set in. To keep meaningless thoughts from racing out of control, I used my mnemonic systems to memorize every detail along the way and then recall them in forward or reverse order. Such a mode of life was not inconsistent with what I'd always known, nor with that of other autodidacts, from obsessed chess players to rogue Latinists holed up in lodgings of extreme frugality all over the Bay Area. Making something of myself was a topic as loudly unspoken as the word Vietnam. I tried to fill the silence by explaining to him my understanding of existentialism, where life has no meaning except what is given to it, a meaning that cannot be authentically measured by some external standard like income. He may have had good reason to ignore such words from a professional plasma donor, and perhaps I should have too, because that's all they were—words. If I were going to interpret things existentially,

I needed *to be in the world*, as Heidegger put it, take some steps, *show* some action. Like Jerry did. That time was getting closer.

•••

It was mid-winter when I dropped him off at the front door of a posh hotel for an after-dinner engagement where he was booked with some new hotshot act that just moved to Chicago. He entered the lobby carrying his prop case like Jesus carrying his cross to the Place of Skulls. I parked his car then came in and sat on a couch outside the banquet room, feeling enormously unhelpful and all too visible, reading Camus's *Exile and the Kingdom*. He decided to play one of those pranks like the kind we used to pull on each other when traveling. Winters in the Midwest are very dry, so static electricity can build up and create a spark if you touch something. Without my seeing him, he approached from the side, sliding his shoes along the carpet to build up as big a charge as possible. Then he touched me on the ear, discharging a loud crackling spark that nearly knocked me off the couch. It burned the words I was reading into my memory like the imprint of a lightning strike: "No one in this desert mattered. Yet outside this desert neither could have lived." My unproductive bookishness must have annoyed him like a shock to the ear. Having gotten my attention, he said, "You aren't going to believe who's here."

My first thought was my mother. I always went up to Milwaukee when I flew in from San Francisco, so she knew I was in Chicago. It would be just like her to find out where I was, then show up unexpectedly and try to whisk me away from my father's corrupting influence.

"Where is she?" I asked.

"She? Look over there. In the powder blue smoking jacket."

I looked into the open banquet room and saw a portly, well-dressed man introducing himself from table to table. He was supposed to be the hot new act in town. Standing with him was an elegant woman adorned with what I was later told were real diamonds. She was not just following him around, but discretely guiding him, making sure he didn't linger too long in any one place as he worked the room. I still didn't recognize him.

He finally had to tell me. "It's Tom Gary."

It had been so long since I'd seen him, I completely forgot what he looked like. I hadn't heard his name since Harvester Show days in the Dakotas and assumed he had dropped from existence along with an endless number of others. I remembered him terrifying people with loud bullwhips that shook the walls of theaters and school auditoriums and often making such a bad impression that he was hissed all the way back to the dressing room. I looked again and tried hard to recognize the blowhard who used to bellow, "If I'd a come low with that whip I'd a taken yer head clean off!"

Everything about him had changed. He was well-groomed and his manner was different, unbelievably different. Instead of a loud slob, he presented himself with the utmost in decorum and finesse.

I watched him move through the room until he approached my father and me.

"Been busy?" my father asked. He didn't say, "How are you?" but "Been busy?" because that was the only way entertainers defined themselves. The question really meant, do you still exist?

Apparently, he did. Very much so.

His escort answered for him. "He's been on the Coast." She was a well-preserved woman of my father's age, formally polite but with more than a hint of hardness. Before any more could be said she chaperoned Tom away, making it clear that if you wanted to talk to him you talked to her first and that it had better be about something important.

When he took the floor that night, I recognized some of his material from the old days, like pulling the tablecloth out from under cups and saucers then shoving it back under. Without the obnoxious bluster, it came off differently. In fact, everything about him came off differently, showing how a strategic change in tone can turn the ear of an ugly hog into a silk purse. The whips were gone, and the jokes that were never funny along with an inventory of new ones all got laughs. It didn't seem like the kind of material he could come up with himself, so I assumed someone wrote it for him.

After his sudden arrival in Chicago, Tom Gary became the glittering object on which all eyes were fixed. Theatrical agencies received calls asking for him by name, as close as a banquet act could get to fame. Two hundred dollars a show was considered top money, and Tom Gary was sold for twice that. He'd work one banquet room, collect his four hundred, then walk across the hall and perform for a different group and collect another four hundred. The next day he'd do a luncheon and then an after-dinner engagement in the evening. He would not have been talked about as much if there weren't performers, mostly outside the Hogan Agency, who remembered him from Harvester Show days. Stories about the old

Tom Gary began to circulate around the Chicago theatrical world, like wrapping bullwhips around faces or the woman in Washington whose family had him arrested for marrying her while she was in a hypnotic trance or the time he turned a coyote loose in a hotel lobby. What they saw now was the new Tom Gary.

He and his mysterious escort, who always answered the phone and handled his contracts, lived in an apartment downtown close to the lake. Rumor had it that he married her somewhere on the Coast. One person said LA, another said Seattle. Some said she was an ex-stripper, others said she was an ex-agent, some said both. They all agreed that she was the one who tamed this rough beast and taught him how to groom, dress, and behave himself. It could not have been any easier than teaching a dog how to talk. What kind of persuasiveness did it take to get someone like him to stop pushing people around? To give up the bullwhips. To mind his mouth. There were plenty of performers who degenerated downward, like Mr. Rhythm or the Prince of Pantomime, but it was quite a rarity to see such astonishing change upward. In the end it was a trajectory that brought him too close to the sun.

The story, as I heard it, was that Tom Gary woke up one morning in his expensive apartment and found his bejeweled handler gone. So was his expensive watch and the money in his wallet. When he went to the underground garage, he found the Cadillac gone too. Their bank account had a balance of zero. She did not leave a note. No one knew why it had happened. It could have been just another case of old-fashioned exploitation, or maybe his training began to fail, like his talking dog that one day decided not to talk. Or it could have something to do with why he had so many ex-wives.

He continued fulfilling outstanding contracts, but they said his performances quickly deteriorated. He started showing up drunk and soon forgot parts of his new routine. He even went back to the whips, something not well received by urbane sales and marketing people under the chandeliers of Chicago's finest banquet rooms. His phone stopped ringing. Then it was disconnected.

He vanished from Chicago just as abruptly as he appeared, yet he was talked about as if he were still the hottest act in town. Someone said he was doing his bullwhip routine again in bars. Someone else said he teamed up with an elderly woman just out of prison and whipped cigarettes out of her mouth in Texas. The stories went on for years because those who spread them wanted them to be true. Beyond the point when he would even be alive, rumors still circulated that he was whipping dimes off people's heads. The day would come when those who perked up at the sound of his name would begin to die off themselves, and the last flickering candle of "Comedy a la Mode" would go out.

CLOSING BIT

THE MASTER SPEAKS

IT WAS NOT THROUGH obligation but an act of filial love that I took on the role of Aeneas and carried my father from the burning ruins of Troy. I couldn't match Jerry's posthumous Purple Heart and other medals, but making something of myself seemed the only way to save my father from his ominous decline. The world outside the dressing room continued to be alien territory to me, and all its paths to conventional success, or even gainful employment, were over terrain that I found impassible. I started classes at the University in Berkeley with the intention of completing my degree but allowed myself to be distracted by misplaced loyalty to a topless dancer from a wealthy family in Burlingame and dropped out again. I came up with other ideas. I imagined bringing him the good news that I was making something of myself as a butterfly farmer. That led nowhere. Then I was going to be a professional genealogist. Then an antiquarian bookseller. I briefly thought I had a future in mnemonic tutoring before I gave that up for the dream of operating a mail-order shoeshine service. As promising as these and other plans seemed at first, they withered in the hot glare of reality. I was about to run out of schemes when I had another idea, the most absurd one yet, but it pestered my mind like a fruit fly that would not go away.

I could do Grover Ruwe's entire act, but I could not make a dummy talk. I knew every nuance of the Prince of Pantomime's routine and could maybe swallow a little harmonica, but playing one was out of the question. I'd been imitating Mr. Rhythm for years with cleats on my shoes, but I could never be a tap dancer. I knew the verbal part of my father's routine as well as he did, but the chances of pulling cards out of the air or picking pockets was vanishingly remote. So, what was the absurd idea that would not go away? It was to poach my father's existential authenticity. In other words, I endeavored to copy what he did—but with restrictions. I knew his repertoire well enough to separate it into components, one being simple things for kids: the Cut and Restored Rope, Card in Balloon, Linking Rings, and a trick with an egg. They took the least dexterity. My thought was to fill in the rest with—what else?—memory stunts. I had already been using mnemonic techniques to get by in all the schools I skipped as well as memorizing physical features along bus and trolley lines to keep my repetitive thoughts from going out of control. It would not take much to put together a routine recalling, for example, a long list of objects suggested by the audience. I would not reveal that I used a memory system just like I did not tell my teachers how I did so well on tests when I hardly showed up for class. And it was not just the simple tricks I could copy, but more importantly the dramatic situations in which he presented them. He'd already worked that out through years of trial and error. I had no illusions of ever performing at venues like Mr. Kelly's or the Copacabana, but I could subsist on birthday parties and church socials, where the standards weren't that high. It would leave me plenty of time to continue my life of reading and memorizing my way along bus and trolley lines.

When I presented the idea to my father, he did not scoff at it like he did my other ideas. It rather appealed to him. In fact, it more than appealed to him. He had suggestions, then more suggestions, until eventually he became a river of suggestions. His letters grew thicker and harder for Chris to wedge under my door. His mood improved, at least on the surface. His inner chambers began to open, and in my weekly collect calls from the hotel lobby his voice became more animated. I heard Jane say something in the background that actually made him chuckle. He even bought a sailboat and took her out on Lake Michigan to relax in the sun, sometimes joined by a comic or crooner from the Hogan Agency, where he was now welcome again at Happy Hour.

Where his gloom diminished, my anxiety increased. An idea was one thing, making it work was another. *Figure it out.* That's what he always told me. So I did. He suggested I start off with "Clippo," a paper rabbit with a long neck that stayed intact when cut with scissors. Good enough for a kiddie party. Anyone off the street could master it in minutes. Of course, the narrative part was an altogether different matter, but fortunately all I had to do was copy his scripting word for word. I did the same with the cut rope trick and the card inside the balloon. There was the egg. And the rings.

In my room I practiced grabbing and thrusting a pillow as substitute for the long-eared creature I would have to live with once again. Even though I knew every word of his routine from seeing it so many times, I was surprised by how much I didn't know, how complicated it could be to coordinate speech, movement, and dexterity in the simplest actions, most of which were unnatural, and make them look natural. I knew from years of memorizing poetry that words can carry layers of meaning, but in this new endeavor words were nothing but flat panels of utility—yet just as essential. In his suit (yet to be altered) with all the false pockets, I did exactly what he did, said everything exactly the way he said it, but could not be further from being him. *Throw your shoulders back and be confident.* It was always good advice for getting me into a classroom where I didn't belong, but it did little for me as I faced myself in a hotel mirror.

His memory feat with the magazine was what distinguished him as one of a kind. Since I already knew and used the mnemonic systems he taught me, he suggested I do that stunt too. It might take somewhat more practice than cutting up a paper rabbit, but it would be easier than learning card manipulations and would set me apart with a unique skill, like simul-talking or spelling any word backward. I set to work on that too. Surely, residents at the Stanley heard me in my room calling out page numbers and headlines that often contained the word "Vietnam." They must have thought I was crazy *because of the war.* In a certain sense they'd have been right.

•••

EVEN THOUGH MY GIVEN name was the same as his, except for the diminutive "Junior" attached at the end, it was clear I had to change it to avoid possible confusion over who was the real goods and who was the knockoff. I came up with a list of names from Russian literature and considered Igor, Viktor, and Ivan as first names, and von Bronsky, Petroff, and Danovitch as surnames. He did not like any of them because they were not populist enough, like "Buddy Jones" or "Joe Harris." When he arranged to fly me into Chicago for my first publicity photos, I wore one of his tailored shirts that happened to have "JP" monogrammed on the cuff and would be visible in the photo. To conform with those initials, I arrived at the last name "Palmer" (derived from the pilgrim who carries a palm leaf back from the Holy Land) and kept my first name, hyphenating it with "Ivan" to give it a metrical lilt. Choosing Ivan (Russian for John) was a private reminder that my essential self was divided in more ways than one.

Now our initials matched. But that was about all.

Many times, I wanted to drop this whole ridiculous charade and reconsider the mail-order shoeshine business, but what would my grieving father do with one son killed in a jungle and the other a stillborn magician and poetry-reading rainbow chaser? How much would he enjoy his sailboat and Happy Hour then? So I persisted in turning myself into a walking photocopy. The terrifying larger question was how do I bring it *into the world of actual existence*?

He brushed aside my concerns about taking on too much too fast, and before I got used to his suit, which was now altered to fit, he set me up with an audition for School Assembly Service, a Chicago agency that booked educational programs like folk singers, storytellers, and puppet shows.

"Everyone has to start somewhere," he said.

"I don't think I'm ready."

"Yes, you are. Hold your head up, throw those shoulders back..."

•••

I FLEW TO CHICAGO and he drove me to a suburban elementary school where it all took place. I borrowed his rabbit, carried in a salesman's case with cat litter on the bottom. A lineup of aspiring programmers was scheduled to show their stuff in a nicely appointed theater before rotating audiences bused in from surrounding schools. We were allowed to do twenty minutes while teachers, advisors, and salespeople from the agency watched and made their assessments.

First up was a fiftyish woman who dressed kids in costumes for a demonstration on the history of clothing. Then a man did a slide show about his trip somewhere abroad. An enthusiastic fellow in a white lab coat picked up a wiener with a pair of tongs and dipped it in liquid nitrogen. Then he shattered it like glass with a hammer. Finally, it was my turn. They introduced me under my new name that made me feel even more like the imposter I was. As I stood at the mic, I froze like the proverbial deer in the headlights. It was worse than walking into the military induction center in Boston.

My mouth somehow began to work and words came out, but they weren't mine. They were his. Beginning with the wine glass from under the handkerchief (I was supposed to say it was Kool-Aid) I robotically said what I'd heard him say my whole life. Then the egg trick, the card inside the balloon, the rings that linked, and the memorized magazine. I finished with the silk scarves and the big rabbit. When I yanked it by the scruff of the neck and shook it in a girl's face, she didn't scream like my father's volunteers. The kids applauded politely and laughed mildly here and there, probably hand-picked and drilled beforehand on how to behave. Somehow it came to twenty minutes, although it didn't seem to have any duration at all. Show time is a time unto itself, within its own realm.

"Not bad," he said in the wings, our places strangely reversed. "Not bad at all, considering it was your first time. You have to remember they won't just sit and watch. You have to *involve* them. Get them to *hold* something, *say* something, *blow* on something, any way to make it look like *they* are the ones making it all work. Stay with it. You'll do all right."

I flew back to San Francisco and waited for School Assembly Service to send me their version of a 4-F classification. Although the rejection would be a great relief to me, I was worried about the effect it would have on my father. After all, I was doing this for him. I'd have to come up with some other way to show I was making something of myself, but I didn't have any more ideas. Each day I expected a terse letter stating, *Sorry, not right for our roster.* Then I heard the sound of a big envelope wedged under my door.

It contained many pages, all assessments of me by salespeople and advisors at the audition. Certain comments stood out immediately: "some of his tricks seemed phony," "not really for all ages," "couldn't hold attention of younger students," "the paper rabbit didn't work well at all," "the magazine part was over their heads." But there were other comments: "liked the rabbit most," "appearance what we want," "really liked the linking rings," "good for this age group," "memory feat impressive." Instead of the rejection I was expecting, they offered me a contract for a thirty-six-week tour of schools in ten states, appearing at up to seventeen schools per week. The money was more than twenty-five times what I earned weekly giving plasma. I'd never seen my father so happy. His worst fears about me were over, and it looked like his only surviving son, the mumbling bookworm who was only good at entertaining himself, would now entertain others (or appear to) and be making something of himself at last.

•••

ONCE MORE I ENTERED THE offices of small-town schools, but in greater numbers than when we'd traveled in the trailer. For all I knew, I could have returned to some of the same ones and introduced myself to the same principals. A certain number of audiences were polite like the ones for the audition, but in the real world of secondary education I faced the constant and unpredictable reality of bleachers filled with little monsters more than eager to eat me alive. As I stood on the gym floor in my father's old suit, reciting his routine word for word, all their wiggly impulses pushed strongly toward chaos. They jeered, they heckled, they threw stuff. The more I directly appealed for cooperation, the more they became sharks smelling blood. If I followed my father's advice and asked a kid to hold something, ten others fought each other for the same chance and the point to what I was doing was lost. During the memory stunt with the magazine, kids screamed the page numbers, hardly understanding why they were doing it. It was the least successful thing that I did, but it made an impression on the principals and teachers. When I produced the rabbit, they rushed the floor and tried to seize it. I could have used Clarabell's handler to keep them back, but I was no Clarabell. Some principals lectured the students beforehand on how to behave, and during my presentation teachers stood and faced them with a burning stare, ready to pull out any miscreants and march them out. But others herded in the student body and left them with me unsupervised. If the principal peeked in the door and saw the hubbub I was up against, he'd write on the stamped, self-addressed postcard that went back to the Agency, "not able to control the students."

I can't say it was entirely their fault. There were assembly magicians like Dick Oslund and Norm Barnhart who were geniuses at staying several steps ahead of the kids and keeping them off balance with an impressive array of strategies I had yet to learn. When I was a student myself, going from school to school, I took what I learned in one place and applied it to the next, so that's what I did now, still trying to win acceptance. Changing how they reacted to me meant changing how I reacted to them. The first thing I did was speed up my pace so they couldn't anticipate what I was going to do next. I made every instance of audience participation contingent on their being quiet and seated. Phrasing these contingencies had to be exactly right because being off by just one word could defeat the desired result. Instead of humbly seeking cooperation (which usually failed) I cultivated a kind of autocratic aloofness, almost to the point of contempt, and to that they responded much better. Improvement began to show when the kids crowded around afterward for autographs. One would tear out a sheet of notebook paper for me to sign. Another kid who didn't have paper would take half of that sheet, and then others demanded half of that until I barely had enough room to sign my name. It didn't matter anyway because they'd lose them before they got back to class. I know because I'd walk over my scribbled aliases on the floor on my way out.

There were a dozen or so other "artists" working through School Assembly Service that season, as well as other agencies in other parts of the country, enmeshing the American school system in a tradition of traveling lecturers going back to the nineteenth century. It was understood, and quite openly, that the real purpose of the assembly was not "educational value," which was what they called it to justify the expenditure, but to get everyone out of class for an hour and relieve the tension that builds up in schools, especially in winter. A blind whistler and a speed typist were scheduled a few weeks before and after me, but we never met as the agency routed us through Moline, Galesburg, Monmouth, Burlington, Macomb, Canton, Muscatine, Maquokata. Then Monticello, Anamosa, Fairfield, Mt. Zion, Red Oak, Clarinda, Wahoo, LeMars, Boyden. Then to West Middleton, Lafayette, Elwood, Winchester, Oxford, Van Wert, Sidney, Marion, Ashland, Mount Gilead. It came to a thousand miles a week. Reading a map and finding the towns (and the schools within the towns) was something I could do instinctively, and at the end of the day, instead of looking for the trailer, I looked for a motel.

Although I was making more money than giving plasma, I had to subtract from my sixty dollars per engagement two separate twenty-percent commissions (one to the agency and one to the salesperson who sold me to the school) plus my travel expenses. Even by staying in the cheapest rooms listed in *Leahy's Hotel and Motel Directory* and eating just the relish tray in restaurants or foodstuffs from a grocery store, what I had left was slightly more than nothing. The value of "mere entertainment."

•••

IF I HAD SO MUCH as an hour free there was no botanical garden, waterfall, or wildlife refuge, no historical house, museum, zoo, or ruins I didn't visit. I did everything my mother wanted to do when she was on the road with my father, which proved that it could be done if there was the will to do it. I saw Johnny Appleseed's grave in Ft. Wayne and a small museum somewhere consisting entirely of paintings on the surface of dried beans. I visited the glacial grooves outside Kelleys Island, Ohio, and the ax murder house in Villisca, Iowa. Instead of lonely kids on playgrounds, I made fast friends with docents at interpretive centers, museums, and historical societies, who tended to be compulsive talkers desperate for someone to listen.

In a town in Illinois that was one block long I met a jewelry maker who showed me how he cut and polished opal cabochons in the basement of his hardware store, where he hardly tended the cash register. At dusk in another town I walked the rabbit on a leash through a city park (keeping an eye out for dogs) and came to a playground where I met a young man sitting on a swing smoking a joint. He told me he worked for a company that sent him out testing for contamination at abandoned gas stations. I was surprised to learn that he used to live in the Haight. Somewhere in Indiana

I met a young woman from New York City who could not find a job teaching second grade anywhere else. We spent an afternoon at a local café talking about T. S. Eliot's fear of cows.

I developed a taste for cheap hotels near railroad depots where trains no longer stopped and were turned into places for the county to put wheezing poverty cases. The lobbies and mezzanines, lit with the lowest possible wattage, often had writing desks and inkwells long since gone dry, and on shelves under them I might even find old copies of *Colliers* and *Coronet* from before the War. They were still the fire traps they had always been, which was why, like my father, I always checked the fire escapes before I turned in. I would sometimes arrive at one listed in *Leahy's* only to find a pile of smoldering ashes. Working school assemblies brought me to so many lodgings in such quick succession that I'd wake up in the middle of the night and have no idea where I was, what town I was in, or even what state. I could not visualize the very room in which I was sleeping, where the door was or the way to the bathroom. All I knew was that I was in a bed somewhere in the dark.

I pursued whatever semblance of romance was possible in this kind of existence, the sort developed by sailors, truckers, pilots, flight attendants, and traveling salesmen. My inamoratas tended to be elementary teachers, town librarians, or thrill-seeking bar types who regarded me as a curiosity, a trip from life in a place where nothing happens. We might exchange letters (theirs sent to me care of General Delivery in different towns and pickup dates), and maybe meet a time or two if I happened to pass their way again, but the novelty soon wore off. They went back to what was more familiar to them, and so did I.

•••

For many years this was my world of adulthood. In time, the school assembly programs would disappear from this world along with the speed typist, the blind whistler, and the wiener smasher, as well as the agencies that booked them. Later in life, shortly before assemblies went the way of the floor show, I married and my wife traveled with me. She was used to old hotels, having been raised in one (since torn down) owned by her father on the east coast of Japan in the little fishing village of Choshi. No more typically Japanese than I was typically American, she became a wanderer in the Japanese diaspora, coming to America via the Amazon and Uruguay, moving from city to city until we met, symbolically, in a tire store. That we were introduced by a bearded and robed Hindu charlatan from India who had taken a lifelong vow of silence might be relevant to the fact that we were three unlikely pariahs on an unfamiliar playground. She easily adapted to my traveling life, and together we sought—and still seek, for its own sake—any seedy hotel that has managed to evade fire or the wreckers, both of us at home with the ghosts that haunt their halls.

BLOWING THE GAFF

AFTER MY MOTHER HAD spent so much money on lawyers trying to get more alimony from my father, there was hardly enough left for food, so the erstwhile lovely assistant, still as animated as ever orbiting people around her, grew dangerously thin and shrank within her elegant clothes. A letter written by a doctor and submitted to the court stated, "the patient is a frail, white female complaining of a sore tongue, allergy to dust, perspiring at night, headaches and frequent moles. I doubt that she will ever be able to carry full time and gainful employment."

Things seemed dire for the ex-actress whose biggest role had been the misunderstood magician's assistant before an audience of judges. Her specialty was storms of mischance, which she never lacked the courage to face. She went through various employments over the next few years, working as a saleswoman at Smartware in Milwaukee, then assistant to an organizer of dog shows, then nanny for the kids of some minor TV actor in Hollywood.

Eventually she became a real estate agent at a company with the preposterous name of Head & Seemann. They gave her all the eccentric clients no one else wanted to work with, like those who would only look at houses after midnight or those who insisted on paying with a cardboard box full of cash. Her photo appeared once again in the *Milwaukee Journal*, this time as part of a full-page advertisement by Head & Seemann, Inc., featuring top agents in their "Million Dollar Club."

The closest she came to reclaiming her lost childhood mansion was a small, pre-War brick structure located within walking distance of where she grew up, which also happened to be near Estabrook Park, the place where she met the enchanting stranger who took her away and locked her in a box. She always kept a room exclusively for me whenever I was in town, laid out like a museum with the receipt for my birth ($188.40), bronzed baby shoes, photos of me next to the trailer at locations known and unknown, a rescued dinosaur egg, my confirmation certificate, and my high school diploma (although I never officially graduated from the first grade). She eventually became too erratic even for the looniest clients at Head & Seemann and had to leave their employment. In her slide into dementia she surrounded herself with ever more chaotic piles of paper, receipts, unpaid bills, articles cut out of the *Milwaukee Journal*, stray currency, and junk mail. One day someone saw smoke coming out of her windows and called the fire department. They dragged a smoldering couch onto the front yard and hosed it down. She had apparently dropped a lit cigarette into a pile of divorce papers, which she tried to put out by stabbing it with a pair of scissors.

Two days after this last dramatic performance she died in her sleep.

Because of my school engagements I barely had time to attend her funeral and go through her things to decide what to save. Living alone, there was nothing to constrain her from filling every closet and cabinet as well as the attic (easily accessible by stairs) with hoarded trash. There was a huge amount of clothing decades out of fashion, some I remember from the trailer, enough to fill the closets of a mansion. But there were treasures, too.

I am now looking at two albums I rescued from her massive accumulation. If it were up to my father, he would have tossed them years ago. Instead, they existed many years in a box somewhere, moved numerous times, and were stored again in other people's basements and garages until finding their way back into her possession and eventually mine. One is from the 1930s, when she first met my father. It contains shots of each of them in rustic settings with captions in her handwriting such as "Bear Lake," "Fascination," "Reflections," "Our First Hike," and "Coffee Eyes." I was surprised to see that at one time they were actually happy together. One anomalous photo shows a circus tent. On the next page I see the image of a woman's shoes filled with sand on a beach. Underneath she wrote "Trickery!" After that a number of photos were torn out with such force that they left a hole in the page.

The other album is from the War and contains undated news clippings from military publications mentioning my father entertaining troops. On the last page is an article from a civilian newspaper after the War, when he was performing in nightclubs. It's titled "Jap Taught Him Tricks." In this article my father is quoted as saying he learned card manipulations in Honolulu from a famous Japanese magician, Tenkai Ishida, known simply as "Tenkai." I had never heard him mention that name.

According to the article, Tenkai was performing in Honolulu at the time of the Pearl Harbor attack. As a Japanese, he was immediately detained under house arrest but allowed to continue performing at a small theater. At the same time my father was on medical leave in Honolulu, awaiting dentures after losing all his teeth from a mouth infection contracted on the island of Roi-Namur, he saw Tenkai perform. He introduced himself and they must have had an affinity similar to what I had for loners I met on playgrounds.

"Tenkai had the ability," my father said in the article, "to transpose cards despite his small hands. I don't know how he did it. Most magicians do pretty well by covering the cards with their hands, but Tenkai had to use his cuffs as well." Even though they were technically enemies, the "ancient Jap magician" and the toothless, left-handed sailor delved into the problem of conjuring with the handicap of short fingers while all around them the world consumed itself in war.

According to other clippings, the arthritic sailor in government-issue dentures traveled throughout the Marshall Islands, sometimes by native catamaran, assigned the relatively safe duty of performing sleight of hand, some of it learned from Tenkai, for troops who might be dead the next day. He conferred upon himself the title "Master of Deception." As part of wartime public relations, he was further assigned to conjure for the indigenous Marshallese, who took his magic literally and sometimes carried him on their shoulders like a god incarnate, no doubt to the relief of his aching legs.

It's hard to tell how much truth there is to that newspaper account. One has to bear in mind my father came from a family of confabulators. His dentist brother told of making house calls at igloos in Alaska. The researcher for the *Dictionary of Regional American English* had her own tales of going into alligator swamps in the Everglades with a tape recorder looking for idioms. His brother William, the millionaire textbook author, claimed to have spent his entire childhood in a tree. My main source for family information was my cousin, the school psychologist. She said my dentist uncle slept with his Eskimo assistants, and one of my unmarried cousins was a lesbian. She said that my father, the "gay blade," once came down with a dose of gleet back in Rockport, but that was just too preposterous for me to believe, just as unlikely as the story of a half-uncle who supposedly fought as a mercenary in the Boer War (the dates didn't match up). My father's code of veracity was simple: "If you make stuff up, you're a liar. You'll get caught sooner or later. If you keep your stories to a basis of fact, all they can get you for is exaggeration, and that's not a major sin. And it's not a lie to say nothing."

I found a photo of Tenkai on Wikipedia that for some reason has since been taken down. Maybe something could be read into that photo and the first one my father had taken after the War. As I hold both photos side by side, I see each in profile holding a fan of cards. Same tux, same smile, same mustache. It's as if he brought Tenkai's picture to a photographer and said, "Make me look like him." My father's smiling face with the false teeth might not have beamed from marquees and lobby cards for the rest of his life if it weren't for the War and the Japanese enemy, Tenkai Ishida.

•••

IN SOME UNKNOWN TOWN, during a quick hour taken from my touring schedule, I listened to an elderly, talkative guide at an historical society explain a display cabinet of World War II bayonets and daggers. She said the museum had the military records of the donors. "All you have to do is make a request to the Department of National Military Personnel Records in St. Louis. But you must be a family member and have their social security number."

I began to think. Since my father destroyed everything about himself, the idea of looking into his dossier from the War seemed like a way to peer into his sealed fortress and maybe find a clue as to whom he was. But I had misgivings. Would this be an honest inquiry, or would I be yielding to the same temptation as those morbid backstage trespassers who put their profane hands on someone else's sacred props?

After much hesitation I wrote to Military Records in St. Louis and requested his navy file. I received a manila envelope almost as thick as some of the letters my father had sent me at the Stanley, but not as thick as the ones I hid for him in the attic. "No Trespassing" was written all over the outside in invisible ink.

According to the documents, a year and a half after the US declared war on Japan, my father joined the naval reserve. In a week he was called up for active duty and assigned to the Fifteenth Navy Construction Battalion in the Pacific as chief machinist's mate in charge of "evaps and purifiers," turning seawater into drinking water. His general build was described as "medium and erect" and the "circumference of abdomen at the umbilicus" was thirty inches. On a page titled "Report of Physical Examination" it was noted that he was not insane, did not wet the bed, and did not wear a truss. He applied for National Service Life Insurance, listing Jerry and my mother (but not Jerry's mother) as beneficiaries at five thousand dollars each in case he should be killed in action. While performing his assigned duty of turning salt water into drinking water on the Kwajalein Atoll, he was promoted from WT1c(CB) to CMMS(AA) (TT)(CB). He was discharged on September 28, 1945, with the rank of chief machinist's mate, whereupon he canceled the life insurance policy.

The discharge papers stated his "usual civilian occupation" as "Stationary Engineer," an elevated title for janitor, but in box twenty-three under "Job Field Preference" it said "Show Business." If he only "preferred" the job of show business eleven years after he left Opal, then what did he do during those eleven years he was *not* on the road as a traveling magician? I always assumed he left Rockport to pull cards out of the air and his wife, Opal, did not want to go with him. But he left Rockport for another reason.

I took a second look at his duty assignments and transfers. While serving in the Central Pacific campaign he was granted a total of one hundred and sixty-four days of sick leave, ninety of those days due to chronic arthritis in both knees. His records frequently mention knee problems, but the stated cause was variously given as "wrestling injury," "falling while jumping track hurdles" or being "hit with a hard object at work." There was no mention of "mystifying card tricks" on Roi-Namur in the Marshall Islands, but military records, voluminously repetitious as they are, contain only what is necessary to process living bodies for war. One of his dental charts states he went to Honolulu for "extraction of natural teeth." Because he grew up before vaccinations were widespread, he seemed to have come down with everything and checked the boxes for diphtheria, measles, chicken pox, and mumps. Something was added to the list in what I recognized as his own handwriting: "gonorrhea, 1930." My cousin's "myth" about the gay blade and the dose of gleet turned out to be true. Venereal disease was common enough at the time, exceeding tuberculosis as cause of death according to a 1927 pamphlet by the American Social Hygiene Society. The same organization reported that contracting gonorrhea "accidentally" from "infected drinking utensils, towels, or similar objects" was twelve percent (sixty percent of syphilis cases in Russia). One reported side effect of delayed treatment for gonorrhea was gonococcal septic arthritis, usually in the knees. None of my father's siblings had arthritis, so it did not run in the family. What was most striking about the added note was the year: 1930. It was the year Jerry was born.

So-called "accidental" infection (as if there were any other kind) can't be ruled out. He could have touched the wrong cue stick or a piece of chewed gum like he always warned me about. However contracted, for a married man with an infant child in a small Baptist town like Rockport to come down with a "disease of vice" must have been trouble of the sort you can't get out of. What do you do? Bewail the wretched water glass? Condemn the damned toilet seat? Whatever the truth, the shame is still there. Medical attention would likely be delayed in favor of the over-the-counter or mail-order remedies readily available to exploit a large market of desperate people (half a million cases annually), but sooner or later—usually later—the infected victim would end up at the doctor's office. Making it even worse in my father's case, the town doctor happened to be the husband of one of his sisters (the philosopher). The situation did not help his reputation as an under-achieving gay blade, married too young and working as a janitor while his siblings basked in the light of their accolades. Medical protocols at the time had to have been equally overwhelming with painful urethral washes followed by smears taken three times weekly until they showed eight consecutive negatives.

One can imagine Opal's reaction to all this on top of dealing with a wailing baby. She must have had her regrets for not letting him jump in the river that night on the banks of the Ohio. He could have actually been an adulterer or perhaps the innocent victim of circumstance. Either way, no amount of explanation could change anything. There was only one escape from the trouble he was in, and that was to split town. After leaving Rockport, he went through eleven years of personal Dark Ages as "stationary engineer" in Milwaukee. Then came Estabrook Park and my mother. Then came the War. Then me.

Shame is not like guilt. It's an ineradicable stain that sets and stays. It discolors personality. Maybe the Hard-shell Baptists of Rockport were right. Beware of John Barleycorn and the temptations of Eve, and what an unforgiving God can do. It explains why he didn't "trust" my exceptionally alluring Hungarian girlfriend. It explains his tolerance for all the shames I managed to bring down on myself. After so many years as a teetotaler, he only drank bourbon and water because it was the only thing he could "trust." Could it be that one fateful night he slipped away from his wife and crying kid and drank something unfamiliar during Prohibition, something he should not have trusted, which led to a lapse of judgment? Anything, as they say, is possible. Riverboats that docked in Rockport had "fast women" of the kind Sophie Tucker warned me about, and there were brothels in nearby Evansville (shut down and later reopened under "medical supervision"). Spirochetes lurked on every surface. *Keep your nose clean...*

I was never completely certain about the ultimate weight of my decision to dodge the draft. Given what happened to Jerry, I could not help but feel I'd abandoned him in the heat of battle. I considered the rationale of conscientious objectors as well as those who dutifully followed orders. Both positions made sense. My own position was simply self-preservation as it was among the 15,410,000 other draft dodgers in a war that became largely discredited.

Since I was looking into secret files, I assumed that somewhere one must exist on me, surely too thick to slip under a door. Using the Freedom of Information Act, I wrote the FBI, CIA, and the National Security Agency, asking for all the material they had on my subversive activities in Boston. Envelopes from these agencies started arriving at my Minneapolis post office box and were forwarded to General Delivery mail drops out in the provinces. General Delivery is seldom used, especially in small towns, so those envelopes with a return address of Federal Bureau of Investigation, Central Intelligence Agency, and National Security Agency must have made postal employees quite curious as to who would walk in and claim them.

The FBI wrote, "We were unable to identify main file records responsive to the Freedom of Information and Privacy Acts request." The US Secret Service furnished the same canned response. The CIA responded with, "We accept your request and will process it." There was no further word. The only document pertaining to my activities came from the National Archives and Records Administration that provided Sheet 16 of the Waukesha County Local Board of the Selective Service System where my name appears on line 21 of a long list of other draftees and the dates they tried to contact me after I dropped out of college and my classification changed to 1-A. In the column titled "Date of Armed Forces Physical Examination" is the notation "Del." for "Delinquent," the only such classification on the list. That was when I took off to Boston with Tyler and the authorities started looking for me. My final classification of 4-F was also the only such notation on the list. Under "Remarks, information concerning dates of appeals, medical interview, volunteering for induction, transfers, decentralized areas, etc." is the reference "Job Number NN-171-145" over which was rubber stamped the word "DESTROYED." The same word was also rubber stamped over all the other names. That was the extent of my "file." No copies of inane letters discovered under the Smith Act, no secret agent reports, no dossier of photos showing me with known Communists. All I knew for sure was that I was alive and Jerry was not.

Thinking conspiratorially, as government agents do, might they have seen my supposed "subversion" as somehow connected to Jerry? I knew about "punitive" duty assignments, and in my own conspiratorial thinking I wondered whether it might be why he was transferred from aeronautical engineer to flying a prop plane barely over the jungle canopy. Nothing was too strange to believe when it came to war, especially the one in Vietnam. When I requested Jerry's file from the Military Personnel Division, it was even more voluminous than my father's, with uncollated sheets covered with the usual acronyms, duty assignments, and medical and dental records. He reported a broken leg from falling down the stairs when he was one year old. There were chronic gastric problems from nervousness over flying the crash-prone F-100 jet in the 1950s. A number of his teeth had been extracted. He sustained minor injuries from a motor scooter accident. Nowhere did I find any reference to a shifty half-brother in correspondence with the Communist Party and seen in the company of Herbert Apthecker, recently returned from Hanoi. His file was purity itself, so pure that there was no mention by name of the country where he was "KIA" (killed in action).

There was a rotating flywheel of questions inside my head. Why didn't Opal mention adultery or VD in her divorce deposition?

Why did my mother claim that my father and Jerry smuggled contraband from Asia in the 1950s when Jerry's assignment there, according to his Air Force records, was "classified"? Why did she tell me once, "At least I wasn't unfaithful"? When my travels brought me around to Milwaukee again, I went into the Waukesha County Courthouse to obtain my parent's divorce decree. Noted on the decree was a "cross bill," an archaic term for a counterclaim, filed by my father. The cross bill, however, was nowhere to be found in the courthouse records. In fact, the entire divorce file was missing. Vanished completely, as if it never existed. I asked the clerk how such a large file could possibly disappear. All he said was, "The records are supposed to be here but apparently they are not. I have no idea why." I hired a private detective, an expert at finding documents, but even he could not locate them. Given the sordid nature of the prolonged proceedings in which my name and those of others must certainly have come up in many a shameful context, it is not unthinkable that someone with an interest in seeing the past destroyed might have a hand in the file's disappearance.

•••

DURING MY FATHER'S LAST weeks alive in a hospital bed in Jane's living room, a few magicians from the local magic society who had seen his photo from time to time in journals like *Genii* or *Linking Ring* dropped in for a visit. What they really wanted was to get their hands on his tricks or whatever collectible material he might have. Since what he did was based largely on hand manipulation and devious psychology, they were disappointed to find that he possessed nothing with false panels and mirrors, no rigged cabinets or cleverly machined devices constructed by illusion makers with underground reputations, nothing of any value that could be hoarded or sold.

In the middle of his minute-by-minute battle to stay alive, a clown showed up. He wore a long necktie with little lights that flashed on and off and a hat on a spring that popped up from the top of his head. My father told Jane to get rid of him, but it was too late, he was already in the house. The clown did some over-the-counter tricks of no interest to my father, who was coughing up copious amounts of phlegm into clutches of tissue. After the clown's silly routine, he asked, "Any stuff you wanna get rid of?" All my father had at that point were a few highly technical manuscripts on card maneuvers written by the reclusive "cardician" Ed Marlo.

"Help yourself," he said to the clown, just so he would leave.

He made off with the manuscripts, which could be resold at a collector's convention for a few dollars. The clown also took the video camera and tripod my father used to study his hand movements from every angle.

•••

AFTER HIS ASHES WERE dispersed in my absence, I flew to Tampa in a break between my non-cancellable school performances to close his safe deposit box. Jane's granddaughter was off somewhere with her boyfriend, a biker who owned a snake. Jane did not seem in the least way grieved, but neither do aerialists the day after one or more of their family members die in a fall. Outward appearances don't have to coincide with what's beneath. As the two of us sat at her kitchen table, she did something she had never done before. She popped open a canned Long Island Iced Tea and poured it into two glasses. Then she lifted hers and said, "Here's to the old boy."

Fair enough, I suppose.

To her he was "the old boy," and to him she was the "tough old broad."

When I opened his safe deposit box, I found a few certificates for limited partnerships in several worthless oil wells in Midland, Texas, and a three-and-a-half carat diamond pinkie ring flawed by a big occlusion in the center. There was a sealed envelope on which he wrote, "Material of interest only to me."

"Open it," said a voice.

"Don't," said another.

Knowing his mastery of misdirection, it might have been a clever setup to draw attention to something he wanted me to see, since he was aware of my uncontained curiosity. *He takes after his mother.* If that was the intention, it worked. I broke the seal.

It was like opening a Pharaoh's tomb only to find it empty except for a few canopic jars and a ceremonial wig. There were only receipts for paid income taxes that went back to 1926. Why, in a lifetime of throwing away anything and everything, was that so personally important? There was one other item, something even more mysterious: a small metal fireman's hat with a tiny perforation for attachment to something like a keychain. A patch of paint indicated it was once red. It had an antique quality, like something very old from another time. I'd never seen it before among his few possessions. I'm sure it wasn't mine. A precious memory from his childhood? From Jerry's? Where and why did he keep it all these years? (Assuming it was a real keepsake. After all, he lived a life of fakery.) That single trinket carried a cathexis as powerful as it was ambiguous.

On the way out of Jane's house to return to the Midwest and continue my engagements as a memory expert, I passed the trash can she put out for pickup. It contained the last clues of his worldly existence: a couple of medical smocks, his Nebulizer, half a shopping bag of used tissues, foam rubber bedding, medicine vials, shaving razor, comb, and a spillage of cards. On top of it all were his false teeth.

END

ENCORES

Bobby Cross: After the Vietnam War was over, one of his neighbors told me he was murdered in a cocaine deal gone bad and that "he did not conform to his family's wishes."

Karen Kiedrowski: When I was still living in San Francisco, my mother sent me a short clipping from deep inside the pages of the *Milwaukee Journal*. It mentioned "Karen Ober, formerly Karen Kiedrowski," whose nude body was found in her bedroom next to that of her nearly nude husband, an ex-bartender sixteen years her senior, whom she planned to divorce. He shot her and himself with a .38 caliber Derringer. Six months later her father died of a heart attack. The entire family—Karen, parents, and brother (but not the sister)—lie in a family gravesite in Holy Cross Cemetery not far from my mother.

Craig Tyler: Within a year after I last saw him, reports came to me thirdhand that his mother had died and he was in prison, but I never knew for what.

Big Brother Jerry: The website for the Vietnam War Memorial came into existence after my father was no longer alive. It was here that I found details of Jerry's death. The account was given by Greg "Doc" Lutes of the United States Marine Corps.

> We had a running gunfight with Charlie to recover his body. I was in on that one. The [pilot, Jerry] observed 4 VC attempting to outflank the CAP 2-4-2 patrol and dived to engage them. The 4 VC initiated [automatic weapons fire] on the aircraft which took an unknown number of hits, crashed and burned at 3.2 km SE of Hieu Nhon District Headquarters. Kind of interesting about the report of him killed while missing. I will not go into the morbid details but he was killed on impact. He saved the lives of the men in that patrol. The patrol initiated organic weapons fire killing one VC in the bunker and one VC attempting to flee the area.

Of the two dead Vietnamese, nothing is known of them or their families.

Grover Ruwe: The ventriloquist miraculously came out of his coma after the car accident and gave up drinking. He took up religion and continued performing with his dummies, Louie and Sunshine, who did not take up religion. He wore a large wooden cross around his neck on and off stage and annoyed everyone with his unrelenting talk about Jesus. Instead of bringing his dummies into bars for drinks, he brought them into hospitals, orphanages, and nursing homes for charity. When he died in a trailer park outside Harris, Iowa, he had two trailers, one for himself and the other for Louie and Sunshine. No one seems to know what became of them. They are not in Vent Haven Museum, in Fort Mitchell, Kentucky, the bone yard for surviving dummies of dead ventriloquists. They may have ended up in someone's possession as souvenirs, or, more likely, found their final repose in a landfill.